Kids & Money

Kids & Money

A Hands-On Parent's Guide to Teach Children About Successful Money Management & Business Basics

by

Michael J. Searls
the creator of "The Allowance Kit"

A World of Money Book

Summit Financial Publishing
Summit Financial Products, Inc.
5350 South Roslyn Street, Suite 310
Englewood, Colorado 80111
1 (800) 513-3779

©1996 by Summit Financial Products, Inc.

Manufactured in the United States of America

Second Edition

Library of Congress Cataloging-in-Publication Data
Searls, Michael J.
Kids & money: a hands-on parent's guide to teach
children about successful money management &
business basics/
Michael J. Searls
p.   cm.
World of Money book
Includes index.
ISBN 0-9648265-8-5: $9.95
1. Children – Finance, Personal.   2. Children's allowance.
3. Saving and thrift.   4. Parenting – Finance, Personal.
I. Title.

Acknowledgments

Nearly three years ago, I was sitting on my deck enjoying the evening, when my daughter, Ashley, came to me with a problem. She was ten years old at the time and explained that she needed $10.00 to go to the movies with a friend. I asked her where the money was that I had given her the day before. "I lost it" was her reply. "No," I said, "you mean you spent it?" "No, I just lost it," she said. Well, needless to say, I dug into my wallet and handed over a $10.00 bill while complaining that she didn't know the value of a dollar.

What concerned me most about this little exchange was not the fact that my daughter had lost the money, but rather that it didn't seem to bother her. She knew that she could just turn to good ole' dad and make up the difference. To make matters worse, I was one of the nation's top Investment Advisors with the country's most prestigious brokerage firm. I handled tens of millions of dollars for my clients, possessed the education and training in finance and economics, yet my own daughter didn't have a clue when it came to money. I began to search for the answer to my dilemma and found only a smattering of books written on the subject of kids and money...none of which gave me the answers I was looking for. My friends and relatives voiced the same concerns as I. That's when I knew that someone needed to do something about teaching kids about money. In early 1995, Summit Financial Products, Inc. and its World of Money line of products (as well as this book) were born. Thank you, Ashley!

I would also like to thank my wife, Lisa. I have never met a woman with so much love, patience and tenderness. You are truly a woman with a heart of gold. Many times I have wanted to abandon these projects and you have single-handedly redirected my course. Without your love, encouragement and understanding, none of this would have been possible. To my children, Ashley, Aaron, Alexander and Austin...any man would be blessed to have children like you. Each of you is so special in so many ways.

Thank you...

to Dan Henderson. You are like a "rock" in very rough seas. Your time, dedication and belief in what we do is irreplaceable. (YGBR!)

to Gary Steele, the smartest Investment Advisor I know. Very few people have the ability to analyze investments *and* communicate with people like you do.

to Chris Turner. Your tireless energy is a wonderful thing to see and be a part of.

to Steve Starr, Donelle Anderson, Aliza Schlifkin and Linda Pimental...you are the ones who really make things happen.

to Jerry Moore, the man who hired me as a stockbroker when I was very wet behind the ears. You taught me more in a short time than anyone I have ever met.

to my parents. Someday I want to be like you!

I also want to thank Larry Bograd for his time and dedication. Without his editorial work, the completion of this project would not have been possible. And thank you to Todd Clary, our superb graphic artist, whose illustrations grace these pages.

Finally, to the parents we serve. You can make a difference...you *must* make a difference!

To Lisa, Forever.

Contents

Introduction

"But First, A Word From Our Sponsor"

Regardless of what they know about economics, whether or not you have taught them to be financially responsible, even if they don't know they're doing it—kids practice business each and every day.

Be a fly on the wall of any school cafeteria and you're likely to hear:

"I'll trade my sandwich for your banana"—here is an example of negotiation and bartering.

"Come on, you know how much *you* like how *my* mom makes a cheese sandwich"—a future marketing specialist in the making!

Other kids are selling baked goods at a table, to raise money for the school band. Or someone is passing out fliers and talking up a festival to be held in the gym over the weekend. Kids are swapping baseball trading cards and sharing leads on baby-sitting jobs. Two kids, having become partners, are targeting potential yard work jobs and customers.

Everyone is talking about how to spend money.

Not that today's world of kids and money is nickel and dime. Far from it. A recent article in *Money* stated that in 1995, the 29 million adolescents in the U.S. collected an astonishing $102 billion (yes, that's *billion*) from jobs, allowance, gifts of cash, savings bonds and other investments. This total has grown $13 billion from just five years ago.

Further, teens spend $67 billion annually and, by directing their parents toward certain products, influence another $42 billion of household spending. This influence includes the parental purchase of everything from cold cereal and movies to the choice of family dining and vacation destinations.

Even kids ages 4 to 12 have enormous financial clout. In 1995, the 35 million members of this age group had a total annual income of $20.3 billion and spent $17.1 billion of it, according to James McNeal, a marketing professor at Texas A&M University. McNeal figures that these young kids directly influenced about $170 billion in family spending.

As the late Senator from Illinois, Everett Dirksen, reportedly observed, "A billion here, a billion there, and pretty soon you're talking big money."

Will teaching kids about money make them greedy? No, I don't think so—kids are handling money anyway. Yet how many children and adolescents really know how to handle it properly? They're learning life skills now, regardless of whether we're teaching it to them. Perhaps they are learning not to care about money, to fear it, feel guilty about it, or to be greedy; basically, they're modeling whatever they see their parents doing.

How many parents avoid teaching their offspring the principles of economics and smart money management?

In how many households is "money" a dirty word, never to be discussed in public and certainly never in front of the children? "Money is the root of all evil," goes the familiar saying. (Which, by the way, is a mis-quotation. The original Biblical passage in *I Timothy 6:10* says, "The adoration of money is the root of all evil." It's the single-minded adoration of money, not money itself, which is frowned upon.)

How many kids have a clue about how much their parents earn? And how much the house or car cost?

Could the lack of attention toward teaching kids about money explain the high rate of financial illiteracy among adults?

According to *Newsweek*, bankruptcies have more than doubled in the past decade, to 837,797 in 1995. The national savings rate is less than 4 percent, down from more than 7 percent in the 1970s.

As in other areas of life, children learn financial behavior by watching what their parents do. Sadder than how financially ignorant most children and young adults are is how financially ignorant their parents are.

How many times have we grown-ups sat down to make a household spending budget—only to disregard it when we wanted something we really couldn't afford?

How many of us are putting away a set amount every week or month for the kids' college *and* our own retirement? How many of us start a college fund for our kids or a retirement fund for ourselves—only to raid it from time to time when the credit card bill is higher than our checking account balance?

Granted, many American parents have no choice but to live from paycheck to paycheck. Wouldn't it be nice, though, if our children never have to do that because the principles of money management were instilled at an early age.

For many years, I was an investment consultant, working with a number of clients and many millions of dollars. I bring this up only to relate an observation: The really successful people tell me that they were taught how to handle money wisely from an early age; those people who simply inherited a lot of money without first being properly prepared often watched helplessly as their fortune dwindled away.

Eighty-five percent of what we know about money is taught to us by our parents. Yet most parents say they don't know enough about money. If this is the case, and I believe it is, why not adopt a system that will take the guilt and the greed away? Why not give our kids a system by which they can manage their money today in a way that makes sense, one that will provide a life skill which they can practice for the rest of their lives? *Kids & Money* will give you that system.

Many parents say, "My kindergartner is too young to handle money. We give her a dollar and she immediately loses it."

Yet, psychologist Ray Guarendi told *Working Mother* that age six is a good time to introduce a regular allowance. "This is the best tool for teaching kids to be smart money managers. It gives them first-hand experience budgeting, saving and making spending decisions."

Financial educator Janet Bodnar, writing in *Parents*, agrees that "between the ages of seven and ten, children develop a grasp of the abstract notion we call money."

Even if parents choose to keep their kids ignorant about the world of money, American companies recognize that very young children have enormous financial clout. Think of the advertising, promotions, and products specifically geared to the preschool set.

Everyone knows that Saturday morning network TV has almost as many commercials selling cold cereal, candy, and toys, as it has cartoons. Because of this, many people insist that their children watch only public TV, so the kids aren't "polluted" by consumerism. Fine, but ask preschoolers which diaper company supports *Barney And Friends* or which retailer underwrites *The Puzzle Place* and you may be stunned when they snap back the answer (Kimberly Clark's Huggies and Sears).

So it's never too early for a child to start learning about the world of finance. Certainly by the time a kid becomes a teenager, if financial discipline is not part of her or his personality, it may be too late. If kids learned the unwise management of money growing up, then those lessons may stay with them forever. No responsible parent would send a teenager out in the world without an understanding about drugs, sex, drinking and driving, so why wait another day to help create financially responsible, financially smart kids?

Who knows, maybe along the way we grown-ups will pick up a pointer or two!

Teaching kids about money will bring out the best—and the worst—in you. Young children may be slow to grasp certain financial concepts or be resistant to change in the domestic status quo. Older kids, used to getting what they want, may view your help as parental intrusion or a boring waste of time.

And opening yourself up to kids' questions and criticism about your own financial habits may push all sorts of emotional buttons. As the famous economist John Kenneth Galbraith observed in *The Age of Uncertainty*, "Money is a singular thing. It ranks with love as man's greatest source of joy. And with death as his greatest source of anxiety."

It's a sad fact that most marriages break up over disputes about money. Almost all of us remember our parents fighting over household finances, even if they remained happily married. The newspaper, TV, and movies are filled with stories of greed motivating all sorts of destruction.

On the other hand, teaching kids about money is a crucial parenting responsibility, and can be fun. Kids delight in learning. Kids delight in pleasing their parents. And we delight when our kids master new information and skills.

The important thing is to keep your sense of humor and to remember that you're teaching your kids something they can learn only from you.

The first section of *Kids & Money* presents the World of Money financial management system, which is based on the simple principles of Spend/Give, Save, and Invest. This system works, whether you're five years old, fifteen years old, or fifty-five years young.

Subsequent chapters help parents teach these principles and other important financial information to preschoolers, grade-schoolers, and teenagers.

Section Two tells how to help your kids start their own businesses—because why should Bill Gates, Warren Buffet, and Mary Kay have all the fun? We're always telling our kids that they'll have to support us in our old age. The least we can do is point them in the right direction!

At the end of the book is a list of resources you can turn to for more information.

Like other lessons about life, learning about money should be serious business. But it should also be fun, which is what *Kids & Money* strives to be. After all, what could be better than all of us laughing our way to the bank!

Section One

Teaching Kids About Money

One

The Allowance Kit System

In many households there is no more painful ritual than the weekly allowance—assuming that the parents remember to "dole" it out.

With hand out, palm open, and head lowered, the kid says, "Ah, Mom, Dad, sorry to bother you. But it's Saturday. Time for my allowance. Remember?"

Mom and Dad do a quick, non-verbal consultation. Should we part with our hard-earned cash? Were the kids sufficiently deserving this week? Did they do their chores and generally behave themselves? Will they love us more if we give them a few bucks to blow on junk food, stupid toys, ugly costume jewelry, and horrible noise which only they could call music?

Begrudgingly, feeling trapped, Mom or Dad opens the wallet and parts with a precious few dollars.

The kid forces a smile, quickly pockets the cash— and doesn't leave well enough alone. "Mom, Dad, I was hoping to get a little extra this week. There's something I'd like to buy."

Dad and Mom look at each other again. Where did we go wrong raising such a spendthrift! Money goes through these kids like water through a sieve!...but is it worth fighting over a few lousy bucks?

So Mom or Dad unhappily surrenders another dollar or two. The kid, who believes that his parents are Mr. and Mrs. Ebenezer Scrooge incarnate, sulks away. Everyone is anxious and resentful, because there's no fair and consistent system in place.

Well, fear no more.

How Much, And When To Start?

For kids to learn how to handle money properly, they'll need a source of income—in other words, their own money. Until kids are old enough to start earning this income by working, an allowance may be their only source.

For starters, though, the country seems divided on whether kids should receive allowances at all. In 1993, the business journal Simmons reported that nearly 50% of children aged six to fourteen received no allowance, almost 37% received an allowance on a regular basis and the remaining 14% received money as needed.

Every family has to make its own decision, but money management can't be learned in a vacuum. If you want to teach your kids how to wisely spend, save, and invest money, then giving them a regular, weekly allowance is a good place to start.

Although almost every child-rearing expert agrees that children should receive a regular allowance and that getting an allowance is the best way to learn how to handle money, there is little agreement as to what age allowance should start and at what amount.

Some people begin when the child starts asking questions about money and what things cost, which may be as young as three or four years old.

Adriane Berg advises in *Working Mother*, "The sooner you begin, the better. When children are young, they're eager to please and to learn. So you want to try to introduce good money habits early on, when kids are still easy to reach." Giving money to a three year old may seem a colossal waste of parental funds, but what's a few bucks if you're starting your kids off on the right path?

Oh, the beancounter inside of you may squawk, "Why should I give a preschooler as much as a dime? He'll just lose it—or, worse, swallow it! It'll end up jamming the washing machine or breaking the vacuum cleaner!"

But how are kids going to learn how to manage money if we don't give them any? Would you rather your four year old lose a dime on occasion or have your teenager, due to financial ignorance, put the whole family into a financial crisis?

By having her own income when she is young, your child will be able to make mistakes while the cost is low. And she—or he—will make mistakes with money. Don't we all? The best way to learn is through trial and error.

By setting a specific allowance amount and sticking to it (more than once in this book you'll hear the refrain: No Advances!), your child will start to learn about the limitation of available funds and about the necessity of staying within a budget.

Once he or she understands the overused adage, "Money doesn't grow on trees," the child will begin to understand the cost of things. When a child starts to spend his or her own money, and while still desiring every item on the toy store shelf, she'll realize that a dollar—*her* dollar—can stretch only so far. The instant a child is forced to start making purchase choices based on comparative costs, a smarter consumer is born.

Remember emptying your piggy bank and taking the piles of coins and the few crumpled bills to the store to buy yourself a model kit or a special cap or some goldfish or, if you were truly industrious, your own bike? Remember the swelling of pride, the sense of accomplishment?

Kids *do* tend to appreciate more the things they buy with their own money. Birthday and Christmas or Hanukkah presents are wonderful to open, but how many end up misplaced or ignored in a matter of days? But let a kid buy something with his or her own money and it becomes something treasured.

Every family needs to make its own decision, but the recommendation is not to wait much past a child's fifth birthday. Why? Because, as a parent, you have only a few precious years to teach wise money management skills to your kids.

Janet Bodnar, a widely regarded expert on children and money, told *Parents* that kids take direction from their parents until approximately age ten; after that, peers become the major influence. Thus, you'll be doing your child a disservice if you wait too long before starting his or her allowance.

As to "How Much?," well, here, the experts show more disagreement. Some say a dollar a week is more than enough until a child reaches third or fourth grade. Others say a kid won't understand the depth of money management if she doesn't have enough to enjoy, save and invest, and to learn mistakes from.

14

Surveys find that six- to eight-year-olds receive an average of $2.00 a week, and that nine- and ten-year-olds receive an average of $4.25.

Here again, family finances, tradition, and practices should guide the answer to "How Much?"

In my family, for example, the kids receive a dollar for every year of age. My eleven year old receives eleven dollars per week, my eight year old receives eight dollars per week, my five year old receives five dollars per week, and my two year old receives two dollars per week. Sure, there's complaints that my eleven year old gets more, but as kids get older they want more, and more expensive items. Besides, that way everyone gets a raise on his or her birthday.

There is a catch. Unless they do odd jobs, the allowance is *all* my kids receive. No hitting me up for candy money when we go to the store. No "free" popcorn at the movies. Of course, if my wife or I wish to treat them, we do. But the irritating "quarter here, dollar there" days are history.

And no advances! If one of my kids wants to buy an item *now*, then they can earn extra money around the house or, better still, learn to save more of their spending money.

Still, a dollar a week for every year of age? Ten bucks a week—to a kid? The beancounter inside of you may be clutching your chest. *In my day, I got a dollar, period—and that was after walking the three miles home from school in the snow!* Well, what did a candy bar cost in our day? A pack of trading cards? A ticket to a movie matinee? Things *are* more expensive today, so it's unfair to think your kids can get by on what we received when we were their age.

If kids understand that there are no more hand-outs

at the grocery or toy store, that there are no advances, that (as we'll come to in a few moments) they're free to spend only a third of their income—then a dollar a week for every year of age seems about right.

As Bonnie Drew, author of *Money Skills: 101 Activities to Teach Your Child About Money*, says, "One of the biggest mistakes parents make is not giving enough. Kids need adequate funds if they're going to practice making sound financial decisions."

Allowance & Chores

Should allowance be somehow tied to the performance of chores?

Again, there's disagreement. Some grown-ups view allowance as a salary—in other words, money earned by kids in exchange for doing things around the house or simply by behaving well. Yet overall, most experts, from Dr. Benjamin Spock to parenting guru John Rosemond, advise: "Don't tie allowances to chores."

"Money is for teaching priorities and to shop smartly. Doing chores teaches good citizenship," writes John Rosemond in *Better Homes & Gardens*.

Chores come with being a member of a family. Some of these chores will be specific to kids, such as keeping their rooms clean and making their beds. Other chores benefit the family as a whole, such as taking out the trash, setting the table for dinner, or mowing the lawn.

Everyone needs to help in order to make a household run more smoothly. Everyone needs to help because, as the adage goes, "We're all in this together!"

Because of this, parents and kids should sit down and together decide what chores the kids are going to do and how often.

Many families find that a weekly Chore List, posted on the refrigerator or kitchen bulletin board, helps everyone remember what she or he is expected to do and on which day. Some families change the list weekly, so chores rotate among the kids. Many parents find that letting kids use stamps or stickers to mark when a chore is successfully completed makes the "work" fun, easy to track, and gives the kids proof of accomplishment.

As kids demonstrate that they can handle simple chores, you can ask them to start on more "adult" chores. But don't expect a ten year old to know instinctively how to wash windows or to load the dishwasher—these sort of things aren't in our DNA. To avoid mutual frustration, take the time to do more difficult chores a few times with your kids before sending them off on their own.

On the following page is a sample Chore List, which you're welcome to copy or modify.

In the squares below, write your tasks that must be completed each day for this week. Fill in one task per square. When you have completed each chore, use your stamp to give yourself a high-five! When you are all stamped out for the day, you're home free!

CHORE LIST FOR ....

FOR THE WEEK OF ....

	SUN	MON	TUE	WED	THU	FRI	SAT
TASK #1							
TASK #2							
TASK #3							
TASK #4							
TASK #5							

YES!! HOME FREE!! EXCELLENT!!

While many experts advise allowing kids to earn extra money for non-chore tasks, more and more parenting and financial gurus say, "Don't tie allowance to chores."

The problem is that if allowance depends on chores, a child will grow to resent them and resent the parent holding back "payment" until the job is complete and meets grown-up satisfaction. And what if the chore is only partly completed—does the parent pay a fraction of the allowance amount?

Just as chores are a necessary part of belonging to a family, allowance should be a right—not a privilege.

I suggest that a child should do chores...because she or he is part of the family and a child should get an allowance...because she or he is part of the family.

The World of Money Three-Part System

When your child or teen receives income, whether in the form of allowance, gifts of cash or check, or earnings, the money should be divided among three areas: "Spend/Give," "Save," and "Invest."

To keep the areas separate and secure, World of Money offers its Allowance Kit for kids ages seven to fourteen, and its Allowance Kit Junior for kids ages three to seven. The kits, available at book or toy stores, come with a customized bank with three compartments resembling a set of books that can be placed on a shelf. (For ordering information, call 1-800-FOR-A-KIT.)

Alternatively, you can use three Mason jars with slots cut in the metal lids, or some other type of containers.

Another way to go is suggested by John Messervey of the National Family Business Council. He suggests parents keep a journal to keep track of their kids' money. "Once a week," Messervey says, "write in dates and amounts and show the child how and where they spent their money, how much is left and how much they have in savings."

Although Messervey's system may work for some families, one drawback is that the parents continue to act as the family bankers, instead of kids being fully responsible for their own money. And notations in a notebook hardly compete with real greenbacks and coins accumulating in containers.

Regardless of which system you choose, the principle of "Spend/Give," "Save," and "Invest" remains constant.

Spend/Give

One of the things that kids should learn about money is that it can be fun. A lot of fun. Which is where spending comes in.

One third of all the money they get should go into this category called "Spend/Give." And they can spend this money whenever, and on whatever, they want.

No longer will you, the parent, be subjected to your kid's shameless begging and pleading and overall bad acting in public. Let your kids know that they are in charge of their own spending money—but no advances! Pretty soon they'll learn that this compartment is not a bottomless pit. If they spend like wild, sooner or later they'll run out.

Pretty soon they'll have an answer (the one you hope for) to the question, "Was it better to buy a candy bar which was gone in a minute, or next time would it be better to save some of the "Spend" money so you can afford something you can enjoy over and over?"

Will kids' behavior change the instant they're put in charge of their own spending? There are no guarantees, but personal experience tells me—yes.

Before my wife and I initiated this system, taking

20

the family to the movies became a spending frenzy. The tickets, of course. But it was the kids' pulling us toward the concessions stand which doubled the cost of the outing. Now, with Mom and Dad no longer reaching into our pockets to satisfy the kids' snack whims, the kids ask if they can bring treats with them from home instead of shelling out three or four dollars of their own money.

Will a system of financial discipline stop kids from spending? No way. *Entrepreneur* magazine refers to a 1990 study that found that by age three, about two-thirds of all children are already making verbal requests for products; by age four-and-a-half, 75% of kids are picking items off store shelves.

The study goes on to relate that eight-year-olds spend an average of $3.80 per week, while nine- to-eleven year olds spend an average of $4.80 per week, and teenagers spend an average of $43 each week. (The teenage figure includes big ticket items like electronic equipment, CDs and pre-recorded videos, concert tickets, and clothes.)

Where does this money go? Texas A & M University reports that $2 billion a year is spent on junk food, $1.9 billion goes for toys and games, $600 million is spent on movies, concerts, sports event and other forms of live entertainment, $700 million is spent on clothing, $486 million is left in arcade video games, $264 million is spread across everything else from stereos to cosmetics. In fact, *kids easily spend twice as much money as they save!*

So, while spending part of their own money should be left to the kids, we parents need to help them become better consumers, too. We need to show our kids how to look for bargains and to understand comparative pricing.

21

As Lois Morton of Cornell University told *The Christian Science Monitor*, "Our kids learn consumer behaviors through watching what adults do." She goes on to suggest, "You could begin by asking your children why they want [a certain toy] over another—comparison shopping." You'll also want to look at which stores have the best prices. One easy teaching tool is to help your kids look through the Sunday newspaper for sales and clipping coupons as a way to break the habit of always going to the same store. Sometimes it's worth driving a little further or making a few calls, to save a few dollars.

An even deeper lesson is possible once kids learn to suppress the I-want-it-I-want-it-now impulse. As one mother told KQED-TV's Susan Kleinman, her nine-year-old daughter "bought enough junky stuff when she first started getting her allowance to learn very quickly what was and wasn't worth spending money on. She has learned to differentiate between wanting something and really needing it."

This story also illustrated a lesson for parents. Kids *will* learn from their own mistakes when we aren't breathing down their necks about how they should be spending their own money.

Remember this section is not entitled *Spend*—but *Spend/Give*.

Just as children learn to spend from observing their parents, they learn in the same way whether or not to be charitable.

As a species, we value generosity. The aggressive business tactics of men like Rockefeller, Frick, and Carnegie may interest historians, but most people remember their philanthropic activities: how their fortunes were left to build universities, libraries, and museums.

If we believe in the future of the human race we believe that people, especially when young, have a heart. It's true that young people dream about helping endangered species, of stopping homelessness and hate, and saving the world. Almost every kid is willing to part with her pennies if it means helping someone less fortunate. How many kids, shopping with their parents at Christmas time, will stop and ask for money to put in the Salvation Army kettle?

In a time of reduced government and corporate support for social services, environmental protection, and the arts, it's up to individuals to sustain these causes and others.

Fortunately, most Americans are innately generous. Many families give a portion of their income to their church or synagogue. Many people volunteer their time and expertise; others donate services and goods. So, without resorting to the "There are children starving in India" approach, remind your kids that they—we—are very lucky to be living in a prosperous country and that we should contribute a part of our high standard of living to those in need.

Simply put, giving returns. Giving makes the recipient *and* the giver feel good.

It doesn't matter whether you direct kids toward the charities which you already support—or help them identify worthy causes and organizations that interest them. What matters is helping them understand that "Spend" is best when it's part of the same breath as "Give."

Save

The second component of the Allowance Kit money management system is "Save."

23

Most of the things kids want to buy cost more than one-third of their weekly allowance. A bike, for instance. Or a new video game. Maybe a pet lizard. Or a pair of those pump basketball shoes. Maybe even a pet lizard that wears pump basketball shoes.

Seriously, one way to help your kids learn to save is to sit down and help them establish a tangible goal. Something to buy with their own money. If it helps, have them cut out a magazine or catalog picture of what they want, to serve as a friendly reminder that savings has a pay-off.

Waiting for money to accumulate until there's enough to buy something expensive is not easy for kids. It's not easy for parents, either. Kids see parents putting purchases on credit cards and moan, "How come *you* can have it now and I have to wait?"

Remember, your kid is learning how to manage life mostly by watching you. As the American novelist James Baldwin noted, "Children have never been very good at listening to their elders, but they have never failed to imitate them."

One mind-set we as a culture must reverse is our resistance towards saving. There's something in the American character which resists putting money away for that "rainy day" or for a computer game program to play when it's too wet to play outside. According to the Federal Reserve Bank of New York, America has the *lowest* savings rate of any industrialized nation!

As with most behavior habits, money habits are easier to change when people are young. Establishing a pattern of regular giving, saving, and investing is very important. "Surveys have shown that children who get no allowances receive roughly as much from their parents as children who do," writes Linda Vanhoose of Knight-Ridder newspapers, "but those on a regular allowance learn more about managing money."

Adrianne Berg, quoted earlier from *Working Mother*, echoes this need for parents to take the lead in instilling a new national behavior toward savings. "Schools teach math skills like adding and subtracting, but parents have to teach the tougher stuff, like how to manage money. Parents must help their kids become good financial decision makers. Of course, teaching children about finances isn't a one-time event, but a process that continues throughout childhood..."

At Your Local Bank

More and more banks are starting programs to attract young savers.

Tom Miers of Mid-America Federal Savings Bank, in Clarendon Hills, Illinois, has a very active kids and money program. One unique feature is its fully chartered branch bank that is located in a high school and staffed by students.

The Young Americans Bank, in Denver, Colorado,

allows customers to open a savings account with a minimum deposit of only ten dollars.

When the First National Bank of Pulsar, Tennessee, rolled out a club for kids to open a bank account with as little as $25, nearly 500 youngsters showed up with piggy banks.

Money Management reported in April, 1992, that in a school savings program sponsored by Dollar Dry Dock Bank in New York, more than 8,000 kids from kindergarten to eighth grade have saved almost $1 million since the program began.

Some banks offer young customers check writing privileges, automated teller machine (ATM) cards, credit cards, and loans for college or to start their own business—the full range of services offered to adults. *My nine year old getting cash from an ATM!*—the thought would cause most parents to shudder. Don't worry, these programs for young customers require active parental oversight.

Next time you go to the bank, bring the kids along. Explain to them that when you use an ATM or cash a check, the machine isn't printing greenbacks and the teller isn't giving you dough because he likes your signature—the money is being withdrawn from your own account. Just as when they deposit and withdraw funds from their account, they then have more or have less of their own money in the bank, depending on the transaction.

If the banks in your area haven't caught on that teaching kids about money management is an important community service, and that kids represent an enormous customer pool—establish a family bank in your own home.

Either pool your kids' money with your own savings

account, keeping track of how much belongs to whom, or agree with your kids on a safe "bank" to be kept somewhere in the house. If you go with a home bank, as an incentive for savings, pay your child the same interest rate currently paid by financial institutions.

Invest

The third and last component of the Allowance Kit money management system is "Invest." It is the most important component, too, because if we do not have "something put away for a rainy day," the threat of debt will always hover above our heads.

Investing can be a challenge for young people because the rewards seem so far away.

To invest properly, money must not be touched for a long, long time. And if a kid thinks waiting a few months for Christmas or Hanukkah takes forever, or waiting a year for her next birthday is a long time, that's nothing. We're talking about leaving money undisturbed for ten or twenty years. Maybe even longer. Talk about delayed gratification!

Yet investing may be the most rewarding part of the Allowance Kit system.

Start by sitting down with your kids and explaining the difference between saving and investing.

For one, savings is waiting to have enough money to buy an item ranging in cost from, say, ten dollars to several hundred dollars. Investing is waiting to have enough money to afford something really, really expensive, like a college education, a house, or retirement.

Secondly, for savings, there are not a lot of choices besides putting it in a bank account, because you plan on withdrawing the money in the foreseeable future.

Investments, because the money is put away for a long time, offer many more opportunities for your money to work for you. But most investments do come with a certain amount of risk. Risk is the chance that your investment may lose money in the short term. Not a happy prospect. But the risk is balanced out because a good investment is more likely to earn a lot more money than a savings account, over the long term.

The notion of money "working" may seem strange to kids. Well, if you leave money for months and months in a piggy bank or stuff it under the mattress, it's not doing anything but collecting dust. If, however, you put it in a savings account or another financial product, the bank or company actually pays you for the use of your money.

Thirdly, discuss your family's portfolio. A portfolio is a group of investments.

For many families, the single largest investment item in the portfolio is their house. Some families own a business, factory or land. Others invest in stocks or bonds. A retirement plan, part of many employee benefit packages, is another form of investment.

Just because something costs a lot of money doesn't mean it's an investment. A car, for instance, starts to lose value the moment you drive it off the dealer's lot. You can't resell clothes for the price you originally paid for them. There's no need to discuss the fine points of *depreciation*, but do help your kids appreciate that some large outlays of money do not qualify as investments.

On the other hand, a house hopefully grows in value over time. A stamp or coin collection, or sports trading card collection, kept in excellent condition for a long time, generally increases in value.

Lastly, some forms of investments aren't tangible.

An investment can be defined in terms of one's time and purpose. For example, a good education is a form of investment because it allows an individual a fuller, richer life. On balance, college graduates earn a lot more money than people who only finished high school. And high school graduates tend to earn more than those students who drop out. There are exceptions, but very few.

Whatever their form, investments are made now to afford a better future.

There are many financial investments open to kids.

Previously, we discussed savings accounts. But banks also have other investment "products"—money-market accounts and certificates of deposit.

Money-Market Accounts & CDs

Money-market accounts pay higher interest rates than normal savings accounts. However, they usually carry higher minimums of deposit and have stricter rules governing how often a customer may make a withdrawal.

A certificate of deposit, or CD (not to be confused with that *other* CD to which you can listen), is purchased for a set amount (again, there may be a minimum) and for a set amount of time—a month, a year, five years. The advantage is that CDs pay an even higher rate of interest than money-market accounts. But CDs cannot be "invaded"; in other words, there are financial penalties for cashing out a CD before its "maturity."

Overall, banks are a good place to start, especially because (and kids will like this) deposits are insured by the federal government. Even if the bank burns down or a thief steals its money, your kids' funds are safe.

Stocks

The stock market and mutual funds offer other investment opportunities. Here, the possible gains—and risks—are higher than with bank accounts or CDs—although these "risks" are not necessarily that great and must be viewed in perspective.

Stock is ownership in a publicly traded company. (Privately held companies, like some family-owned businesses, may not issue stock. These companies are owned by one or a few individuals.) An investor may buy a *share* of stock, giving him or her a tiny part of the company.

With stock ownership comes the right to vote in company matters. One can participate as a shareholder by attending a shareholders meeting, and addressing the company's executives and board of directors.

Many companies, particularly those with products geared to young consumers, have special programs to attract young investors, which will be discussed later.

By the age of eleven or twelve, according to Jane Bodnar writing in *Kiplinger's Money-Smart Kids*, about 10% of kids have advanced from savings accounts to stocks and mutual funds.

Bodnar warns that many full-service stockbrokers charge a minimum commission, sometimes as high as $100 or more, to purchase as little as a single share of stock. Discuss with your broker ways to avoid this, like asking him or her about the fees to establish a custodial account. Also, you can try a discount brokerage firm, or bypass brokers altogether by, among other alternatives, joining an investment co-op like First Share (1-800-683-0743) in which members of the co-op sell or buy shares from other members.

Mutual Funds

Mutual funds are a different type of financial product. Here, a person may buy an interest in a number of different companies at the same time by joining his or her money with other investors participating in the same mutual fund.

Mutual funds hire managers to identify companies in which to buy stock on behalf of the customers depositing money in the mutual fund. Some mutual funds have holdings worth *hundreds of billions* of dollars.

Other Possibilities

As the young investors become more savvy, you (or your financial advisor) may introduce them to other possibilities: bonds, commodities, and precious metals.

The hope is that when they decide to sell an investment, it will bring a lot more money than the amount originally put in. For instance, if the real estate market is good, most people make a profit when they sell their house.

The Importance of Good Record Keeping

Regardless of how your kids invest their money, they must start keeping a list, or register, which should be updated whenever a transaction takes place. When statements from banks, mutual funds, or brokerage firms arrive in the mail, take the time to go over them with your kids, and to have the kids update their personal register. For your convenience, there is a sample Investment Register on the next page.

31

DATE	DESCRIPTION	DEPOSITS	WITHDRAWALS	TOTAL

At the least, a register should keep track of dates of transactions, a description of the investment (for example, name of company and how many shares were purchased), the amount paid into the investment or the amount cashed out when sold, and a running total for the year.

The running total represents the current total amount invested in an individual portfolio. The current value can only be determined using the current market prices of the individual investments.

In addition to tracking "buys" and "sells," a more sophisticated register should keep track of splits (when a company announces a "two for one," the number of total shares doubles, which reduces the price of a share by one-half; which, in turn, makes a share more affordable and attracts new investors), dividends or capital gains paid to shareholders or reinvested on their behalf. This latter information should be made available to your tax preparer, if your child's earnings are enough to require him or her to file an income tax return.

Speaking of taxes (sorry, but unavoidable), it's important to note when a stock or mutual fund is purchased and at what price—because, years later, when it's sold, the profit (here, the difference between purchase price and sell price, less any commissions) is subject to capital gains tax.

The point of almost all investments is that one's money must be left in place and not disturbed in order for the investment to grow in value.

Although thoughts of college—not to mention, retirement—may seem light-years away to a kid, find a way to get across the importance of investment.

Shouldn't all of us, like the gentleman pictured below, have something to look forward to?

Rules Can Be Golden

If you and your kids agree upon a few simple rules about allowance, everyone will be a whole lot happier in the long run.

For starters, pick a regular time when allowance will

be paid. This will eliminate a lot of potential begging, whining, hand tugging, and out-and-out arm wrestling. Now, I'm not suggesting that it be as specific as "Tuesday at 2:17 and 35 seconds p.m." But agree upon a general time, like Saturday morning, and stick to it.

In general, at least for kids who are just starting out, getting paid an allowance once a week is much easier to manage than getting paid only once a month. A lot of families also find that weekends are a little less hectic than during the week. (Unless you're in *my* family, when Saturdays are three separate soccer games, lessons, friends' birthday parties, concerts, and this takes us only up to noon!)

Speaking of rules: Remember, no advances!

The whole idea of getting an allowance is for kids to learn how to manage their money. At some point, they're going to run out. We guarantee it. Stand firm, parents, no matter how much they drop their lower lips and complain. If you cave in, then the kids aren't learning anything—other than that they can manipulate you.

Oops Is Part Of The Plan

Mistakes with money are going to happen. Count on it. We parents make mistakes with money. And our kids will, too.

A child should recognize a mistake and you should help him or her to learn from it. But resist the temptation to become furious, judgmental or hurt when your kid goofs up. Because most everyone learns more from an occasional mistake than from events that unfold without a hitch.

Chances are, the more you're involved, in a constructive way, the less likely it will be that your kids will make a serious blunder. As with other areas of life, if your children feel you're open, they will seek your advice and appreciate your help.

One way you can prevent a kid from looting the saving component of the Allowance Kit System is by making regular trips to the bank with him or her. The investing component should be emptied every few months—whenever there are sufficient funds with which to buy stock or add to a mutual fund.

If you and your kids follow the Allowance Kit System, they'll be well on their way to learning how to manage money, which is certainly no small feat. Managing money is consistently one of the hardest things we—grown-ups and kids—have to do.

Discipline is the key. Follow the Allowance Kit System and rules, and you will all undoubtedly experience success. Stray from the guidelines and your kids are liable to find themselves opening up a can of worms, instead of a bank of money.

And remember, it *is* okay to laugh all the way to the bank. Just tell your kid to try not to be too obvious about it.

Two

"You Mean The Store Makes You Pay For Things?"

Teaching Your Preschooler

The scene is all too familiar. You're at the grocery store and it's crowded. Your preschooler is with you and, for the most part, has done nothing more embarrassing than accidentally knock a can off a shelf.

You're tired and in a hurry, and you've made it to the checkout line with a full buggy. Your preschooler seems content, placated by the free cookie which the store gives to kids.

Now it's ten minutes later and the line hasn't budged. The customer at the front, with a buggy loaded halfway to the ceiling, is arguing that the four ounce tin of tuna is on sale, while the cashier politely insists, "No, it's the six ounce tin that's on sale."

You let out a sigh. You check your watch. You know your preschooler can't hang in there forever—and then it happens.

"Mommy, gimme that balloon. I want it. Please, Mommy. I said 'Please'."

Balloon? What balloon? You look around and, sure enough, there's a Mylar balloon decorated with hearts floating above the magazine and candy rack.

"Not today, sweetheart," you say. "Mommy's in a hurry."

"Please. Please, Mommy!"

"I said 'No.' Besides, it costs money and you really don't need another balloon."

"But the store wants me to have it!" whines the preschooler. "I know it does!"

"Honey, it'll pop before we get it home. Or the wind will blow it away," you reason. "You already had a free cookie. That's enough treats for one day. I'm not paying for a balloon."

"Mommy! I said 'Please!' Please, Mommy." Your preschooler has started to cry and wail. "Give me it and I'll behave—I promise!"

The customers behind you are moving their buggies to other lines. The argument over tuna stops, as all eyes focus on you. And you're trapped.

Do you surrender to the whims of your thirty-five-pound boss? Do you hold your ground and threaten a preschooler's meltdown? Do you snatch your kid and make a run for the minivan before the cashier calls the security guard? Is any of this worth one lousy Mylar balloon?

I can't promise you'll never have another scene like this at the grocery store. Or the toy store. Or the mall's food court. Kids will be kids.

But most experts agree, when your child is old enough to start wanting things, she or he is old enough to start learning about money.

Obviously, you can't expect your preschooler to comprehend the finer points of finance. Most grown-ups can't do that! But a child, even as young as three, can grasp the concept of money and start to practice good financial habits—if the lessons are concrete.

Appreciate that it's not only money which is too abstract for most preschoolers. It's a rare four year old who understands other abstract ideas like time and distance. Here's an example, which may sound familiar.

My five year old asks, "How long before dinner is ready?"

"About an hour," I answer.

"How long is that?"

"Sixty minutes," I say. "Sixty minutes make up an hour."

My five year old still doesn't understand. "Is an hour a long time or a short time?"

"An hour is about how long *Sesame Street* lasts," I try to explain.

My five year old looks at me as though I'm trying *not* to answer the question. "Daddy, how long does *Sesame Street* last?"

"About an hour," I say. "That's how long it is before we eat dinner."

"Is that a long time or a short time?"

Suddenly, I'm doing an Abbott and Costello routine with my kid!

The point is, don't expect your preschooler to understand as much about money as older children will. Even when they start to memorize simple arithmetic, like adding two plus two, too much information about numbers or money may simply confuse them.

And there's a lot about money which goes against a

child's (and an adult's) sense of logic. For instance, if a nickel is bigger in size than a dime, why isn't a nickel worth more? How can Mom or Dad use a piece of paper and a plastic card, neither of which looks like money, to buy just about anything?

Since hands-on is the best approach to learning for this age group, what follows are some activities you can do with your preschooler. You'll need to collect a bag of coins, and bills ranging from one dollar to twenty dollars, and the usual arts and crafts supplies like paper, pencils, crayons or markers, scissors, and glue.

Which Coin Is Which?

Show your preschooler the coins most often used in this country: penny, nickel, dime, and quarter. If you wish, include a half-dollar and a dollar coin.

Demonstrate how each coin has two sides, and that each side is different.

There's a famous person (Lincoln, Jefferson, Roosevelt, etc.) on one side, and a famous building or symbol on the other side. The side with the person is also called "Heads" because there's a head on it.

The other side is called "Tails" because it's opposite the head. Sometimes it has a building—like the penny has the Lincoln Memorial because President Lincoln is on the head side. Or the nickel has Jefferson's famous home, Monticello. Other coins have symbols important to our country, like the eagle on the back of a quarter.

Explain how each coin actually has two names, just as people are often identified by several different names (Daddy is also Mike and Mommy is also Lisa). So a penny is also one cent. A nickel is five cents. A dime is ten cents. A quarter is twenty-five cents. A half-dollar is fifty cents. And a dollar is also one hundred cents.

Since preschoolers know that five is more than one and that ten is more than five—start interchanging saying "the five-cent coin" for "nickel" and "the ten-cent coin" for "dime." Soon your preschooler will understand that, even if a nickel is bigger, a dime is worth more cents.

Sort the coins in order of worth. Place a finger on each coin as you repeat its name and value.

Now scramble the coins and have your preschooler try to put them in order, starting with the least valuable and ending with the most valuable. Expect a lot of trial and error at first.

For fun, scramble the coins on a table and cover them with a piece of paper. Have your preschooler rub the paper gently with a pencil until the coin images start to appear. (They'll love this!)

Cut out the pencil rubbings and help your kid arrange them in sequence and tape them to a blank sheet of paper. Finally, write (or help your child write) the name and value of each coin underneath the image.

How Does A Dollar Stack Up?

This activity may be used for preschoolers, as well as for older kids. For younger kids, it's a counting game. For older kids, it's a lesson in equivalent sums.

Make sure you have a container holding an assortment of coins, with at least 100 pennies, twenty nickels, ten dimes, four quarters, two half-dollars, one one-dollar coin, and a single dollar bill.

Put the dollar bill aside. Then empty the coins on a large flat surface, like the kitchen table, and scramble them.

First, make sure your preschooler can identify a penny (or one-cent coin), a nickel (or a five-cent coin), a dime (or a ten-cent coin), a quarter (a twenty-five-cent coin), a half-dollar (a fifty-cent coin), and a dollar coin (which is worth 100 cents). Explain how the dollar coin is worth the same amount of money as the dollar bill.

Start by asking how many one-cent coins make up a nickel. Count out the pennies until reaching five, if necessary. The same for a dime, quarter, half-dollar, and finally, a dollar.

When your preschooler has stacked a hundred pennies (not all in one stack, please!), explain how a pile of one hundred pennies is worth the same as a single dollar bill.

Now try the same drill with nickels. How many five-cent coins make a dime? How about a quarter? A half-dollar? A dollar?

Dimes are next. Dimes are ten cents. So we have to count by tens—not by ones or fives. So you can't make dimes exactly equal a quarter, but five dimes will equal a half-dollar and ten dimes will add up to a dollar.

A quarter, besides meaning twenty-five cents, is also another word for one-fourth. Don't expect a preschooler to understand fractions. But you can cut a piece of paper or fruit into "quarters" and your child can easily see how one thing can be divided into four parts. So there's two quarters in a half-dollar and four in a dollar.

Many preschoolers know that "half" is a part of something. Just like you can cut a sandwich in half, a dollar is two half-dollar pieces.

If you can get a preschooler to understand the different ways to make a dollar, and that a hundred pennies is a lot of pennies, these are big steps.

For older kids, you can use this same activity to help them find different ways to assemble specific amounts of money. For example, think of the various combinations which make up a quarter. Twenty pennies and a nickel, five nickels, two dimes and five pennies; a dime, a nickel, and ten pennies, and on and on.

The Great Pretend Store

Preschoolers love to pretend to be grown-ups. Which explains the popularity of "playing house" and "playing jobs." Kid-scale kitchens, complete with plastic food and utensils, are a staple of almost every basement playroom. Toy stores sell packaged replicas of name brand fast food products.

So, with little effort, you and your preschooler can "open" a pretend store or restaurant, which will help them practice exchanging money for goods. As with the previous activities, the idea here is to make tangible the abstract notions of finance.

You can use play money from a board game, or real money, or even make up your own currency using large buttons and "dollar bills" which your preschooler can decorate.

Give your child a set amount of money and have her or him start "shopping"—or, if a pretend restaurant, ordering items from a menu. Let him or her go wild. If she wants to load her basket so full of goodies that she can't lift it, fine. If he wants to order everything on the menu, warn him about tummy aches but don't discourage him based on cost. When it's time to pay, you can play the cashier and help with the math.

If the cost of the items is more than what the shopper has on hand, politely tell her to select which items to return and which to keep until it's an even exchange of money for goods. If the bill for the fantasy meal is more than he can afford, ask him if he wants to go without dessert (not likely!). Or will he drink free water instead of a beverage which costs money?

This activity, besides being fun, allows a young child to practice staying within a budget.

Second, it shows that spending money is often a matter of deciding what to buy now and what can wait until later—in adult terms, prioritizing purchases.

Chores

Now that we've had some fun, let's move on to the mundane topic of chores.

Kids like to help around the house, even if their "help" sometimes results in more work for their parents. To please you, a four year old may happily make her bed. Afterwards, it may resemble a haphazard pile, but she's still to be congratulated for helping out.

Whether it's sweeping or emptying waste baskets or helping with the dishes, just keep in mind it's the thought that counts. A little parental help after your preschooler announces the chore is "perfect" may be necessary. But it's worth it if you establish the expectation of chores in your kids at an early age.

How To Counter What They See On TV

It isn't easy.

There's a good reason why major corporations spend the bulk of their advertising dollars on TV—it works. It works whether the captive viewer is three or ninety-three years old.

Spend an hour with your preschoolers watching Saturday morning cartoons and after every commercial you may hear, "Can I get one of those?"

Whether or not it's moral for companies to target advertisements toward very young minds so aggressively is open to debate. The reality is, they do.

Every year, four million births are added to this country's kid population of 45 million, which may explain why there are over 36,000 retail toy stores in the United States.

The prime way for advertisers to reach preschoolers (and the rest of us) is through commercial television. All of us—all of us less-than-perfect parents— have from time to time used the "boob tube" as an electronic baby-sitter. We feel guilty about it (well, maybe not *that* guilty), but it buys some time in the afternoon to start dinner or on Saturday morning to start some laundry.

Not being totally irresponsible, we screen the programs for "scary stuff," but rarely do we interfere when the commercials come on.

One way to make your preschoolers smarter consumers is to watch the commercials with them and, the next time you're in the toy store, show them the actual product. Will the toy or game which looked so amazing on TV be anywhere near as great in real life? Let your child answer this for him- or herself.

Another trick that TV advertisers use was spotted by Carolyn Hoyt, who writes in *McCall's*. "Commercials emphasize the word *only*. But if the toy train set costs 'only' $40, but it's not complete unless the child also springs for batteries and the miniature buildings and people, it will surely bring her nothing but frustration."

Keep in mind that the preschool mind, while sure of its wants, is just starting to understand what money is and what it can do. On the other hand, there's no reason why lessons on smart money management and consumerism can't start well before your child can read or write.

Some areas of a preschooler's intellectual development must wait, like (for most) reading and writing.

But, since preschoolers are all able to say, 'I want' and 'Gimme', there's no good reason to delay their financial education, which includes starting them on an allowance before they're ready for kindergarten.

Hey, isn't it worth it, if it avoids a scene in the checkout line?

Three

"But All Of My Friends Get To Buy It!"

Working With Grade-School Kids

By the time your kids turn ten, you are no longer the most important influence on their financial habits. As scary as it may seem, they are now more likely to follow the leads of their peers than to follow your direction.

So it's crucial that you continue to teach your kids in the early primary grades.

Particularly in grades kindergarten through second, kids are very eager to absorb new knowledge, but their attention span can be frustratingly short.

They love to make up their own minds, but making choices may become an ordeal for them *and* their parents. I suspect the following scene may be all too familiar.

You tell your first-grader that she can take a dollar of her own spending money when she accompanies you to the grocery store after lunch. She wants to buy a chocolate bar. Fine.

Then, when you reach the candy aisle, suddenly she's stricken with consumer paralysis.

"Both the plain one and the one that's crunchy look good," she says. "Can I buy both?"

"No. Just one."

"But Meg's mom buys her both!"

"That's between Meg and her mom. You and I decided you could spend your own money and buy one candy bar. So which is it going to be?"

"I can't decide," your first-grader sighs. "I bet they both taste good."

"Life is choices," you tell her—which hardly consoles her.

Twenty minutes later, she's still deciding. The ice cream in your buggy has started to melt. You've lost your patience. You want her to make her own decision—but choosing a chocolate bar hardly qualifies as a life-or-death choice.

Welcome to the often contradictory world of grade-schoolers.

Money is very important to grade-schoolers; at times, an obsession. So why are they always losing it? Why are they seemingly incapable of emptying their pockets of coins and crumpled bills before dropping their dirty clothes in the hamper?

As opposed to preschoolers, kids in the primary grades understand that today's choices affect tomorrow's outcomes. So why do they spend their own money on worthless junk in which they almost immediately lose interest?

When third or fourth grade rolls around, suddenly you become the ogre standing between your kid and peer approval.

Everyone else is sporting $60 athletic shoes—why can't your kid? Everyone else gets *new* in-line skates and *new* baseball equipment and the latest designer clothes for the teeny-bopper set. Will you join the consumer frenzy or do you want your kid to be a total social embarrassment?

At age eleven or twelve, when allowed to go to the mall with their friends, expect your kids to be the target of sometimes friendly, sometimes not-so-friendly pressure to spend every cent they bring with them.

Certainly, as they get older, their needs and demands become more expensive. You may spend twenty dollars on a video for your preschooler, but she will watch it dozens of times before becoming bored with it. On the other hand, what twelve year old wants to wait for the movie to come out on video? No, she *needs* to see it, with her friends and preferably more than once, and then buy the video the day it's available.

The silver lining is that by the time your kid reaches the age of ten or eleven, he or she can start earning some money by doing jobs at home or around the neighborhood. Keep in mind, though, that there are laws governing work by minors.

The law states that no one under sixteen years of age is allowed to do "hazardous" work.

If a person is under fourteen years of age, technically she or he can only be employed by parents.

The law does *not* say, however, that a young person cannot be self-employed.

Anyone under age fourteen is not supposed to work more than three hours on any school day, eighteen hours during a school week, and eight hours a day during a vacation.

Because some states have even stricter laws than these examples, you should contact your state's Department of Labor or Office of Employment to see what your child can and cannot do.

For some money-making activities attractive to teenagers, like starting a yard work operation or opening a food service, they may need a special license or permit to operate the business. Here, check with your city government.

Some parents obtain a Social Security number when a child is born. Certainly by the time your kids start earning their own money or start to invest it, they should have a Social Security number. If you have questions, you can contact Social Security directly at 1-800-772-1213.

If your kids make enough money, either through wages or investments held in their name, they may be liable for federal and state income tax, regardless of their age. Check with your tax return preparer, or call the Internal Revenue Service at 1-800-829-3676.

If you and your eleven or twelve year old decide it's time she starts earning her own money, don't send her unprepared out into the working world.

A logical first job is taking care of children, either as a mother's helper or baby-sitter.

A mother's helper is one helping the hiring person while she or he remains in the house with the helper. It's easier for the parent of a toddler when there's an eleven year old present to distract the youngster.

A baby-sitter is expected to take care of children when the children's parents are away from the house.

If your daughter (or son) wants to baby-sit, first have

her (or him) complete the Red Cross Baby-sitting Class, which is open to kids eleven years or older. Call your local Red Cross Chapter for information.

If your kids want to wash cars, let them start with the family car so they can get the hang of it.

I'll discuss how you can help your kids start their own business in section two. The point is, by the time your kids reach double-digit ages, expect them to augment allowances with money earned on their own.

An advantage to teaching money management to kids older than preschoolers is that their world is opening up. By kindergarten or first grade, they're wondering about the natural world and how things in the human-made world work.

Since money is such a fixture in our day-to-day life, kids may not realize that it wasn't always around—that, in short, money had to be invented.

The history of currency is fascinating and itself the single subject of many books.

A Quick Exchange On Money

The date is impossible to pinpoint, but when ancient people began to need things from each other, business was born. Berries were traded for feathers. Feathers were swapped for fish. Fish were exchanged for skins. Before the invention of money, this system of barter was used.

Bartering is one of the first interpersonal skills a child learns. Kids know that if they do certain things they will be rewarded.

"If you finish your dinner, you can have dessert," the parent offers.

If the kid wants ice cream, he'll barter for it by eat-ing every bit on his plate. Kids trade toys. They trade shoes and clothes. They grow up hearing stories of business transactions. Every kid knows that Jack traded a cow for a bag of magic beans.

In *The Story Of Money*, Betsy Maestro traces the origins of commerce to when humankind developed agriculture, and permanent settlements became a necessity.

Villages brought together people needing different things. Individual providers were needed by the community, like millers to grind grain into flour, and potters, weavers, toolmakers, carpenters, and other tradespeople. Agriculture produced surplus crops, which would be exchanged for goods.

Over time, villages designated certain days as market days, when the community gathered in one place to exchange goods and services.

Some necessary items were not easy to come by. Salt, for instance. Therefore, salt became one of the first forms of money. In certain parts of the world, people began to trade salt—and certain spices—for goods and services. In other parts, shells, tea leaves, blankets, and grain were used as money.

The problem with these items, though, was that some could spoil and some were too bulky to carry.

People needed something that was easy to handle and, at the same time, was viewed as worthy to exchange in trade.

About five thousand years ago, the people in Sumer, in what we call the Middle East, began to use metal silver as money. Sumer was located in what is now Iraq, between the Mediterranean Sea and the Persian Gulf. The Sumerians melted the silver into bars, which were stamped with their exact weight.

The Sumerians are credited also with inventing the

wheel and the sailboat, which greatly widened their influence, and widened the acceptance of metals like silver and gold as money.

Coins were first used about 2,700 years ago. In 640 B.C., the kingdom of Lydia, which was located in present-day Turkey, issued tiny coins stamped with a lion's head, which was the mark of its king. Other coins followed, and were accepted as long as they were made of precious metals.

Paper money seems to have been invented by the Chinese, long before the explorer Marco Polo brought the idea back to Europe with him in 1295. Each paper note, or bill, was guaranteed by the country's leader to be worth a pre-determined amount.

Europe, however, would not use paper money widely until 1661, when Sweden became the first country to print it.

If you take the kids to Washington, D.C., be sure to visit the Bureau of Engraving and Printing, which makes our paper dollars. (This branch of the U.S. Mint also prints savings bonds, government checks, and postage stamps.)

If you're in Philadelphia or Denver, visit the Mint located in these cities, where coins are made and shipped to banks across the country. (The Mints also make coins for other nations.)

By the way, the word *bank* is Italian and comes from the Italian word *banca* which is the counter or bench where money is laid out.

Dollar has a more complicated origin. In 1518, a large silver coin was minted in the Bohemian town of Joachimsthal. The coin became known as a Joachimsthaler, which was shortened to *thaler*, which in English became *dollar.*

Coin Collecting

I bet many of you wish you still had the coin (or stamp or baseball trading card) collection you so diligently kept as a kid!

Starting when they're in first or second grade, kids are old enough to start a hobby. Kids love to collect things, and collecting coins is a great way to introduce them to the world of money—and a better-than-average investment if you help them take numismatics (coin collecting and study) seriously.

Every town has coin clubs, many of which welcome young members. Ask your local hobby store, which will probably point you in the right direction.

As kids go through the primary grades, they'll be expected to show increased proficiency in arithmetic.

Use the following activities not only to make them smarter with money, but also to practice and sharpen math skills.

Cut & Paste Budget Planning

Earlier, on page 24, I suggested that kids find magazine or newspaper pictures of things they wish to purchase, to create a visual "wish list."

This activity begins with your kids assembling a collage of things on which they would like to spend their own money—sports equipment, movies, toys, whatever. Put no limit on the number of items. As with wishes in general, the sky's the limit.

If prices for the "wish list" items are not evident, help your kids estimate a likely amount.

Now, give your kids a set amount to spend; say, a hundred dollars.

Have them add up the total cost of their "wish list." My guess is that the total will easily exceed the hundred dollar budget.

What items are they willing to forgo, at least for now, to bring the total spending under budget?

Besides practicing math skills, this activity is a lesson in how to prioritize spending. If more adults practiced prioritized spending, there would be a lot less consumer debt and bankruptcies in this country!

When Less Is More

Thanks to consumer activists, grocery stores now display the "sticker" price as well as the unit price on the shelf label below individual items.

Cereal is priced by the box *and* by the ounce. Aluminum foil is priced by the roll *and* by the foot. Unit pricing allows consumers to comparison shop.

Next time you're at the store with your kids, ask them to decide which brand of fruit juice to buy—the one that costs $1.85 for 24 ounces or the one that costs $1.50 for 20 ounces. (Answer: the 20-ounce container is two cents an ounce cheaper.)

Of course, more often than not, the larger the container, the cheaper the unit price. Laundry detergent, for example, gets less expensive by weight as the box size gets bigger. But, again, have your kids do the math and tell you which size of your favorite brand to buy.

How Much Is How Much?

It seems that department stores are always offering "big sales." One reason is that department stores are always moving merchandise on and off the floor. Every season there are new fashions. And during every season, there are several holidays with special merchandise. Spring begins with the end-of-winter clearances, making room for short-sleeved shirts, blouses, and dresses in lighter fabrics. Spring also brings Easter, Mother's Day, and Memorial Day, each of which offers the store a holiday tie-in.

Summer brings pool and beach wear; the Fourth of July sale and, starting in early August, the all-important back-to-school surge.

Autumn starts with the enormous Labor Day sale, to clear out what's left from spring and summer and to make way for the fall fashions. Autumn brings Halloween, which now marks the start of the important end-of-the-year retailing period that includes Thanksgiving and Christmas.

Because of this enormous turnover of merchandise, stores are always offering "marked down" items, usually in the form of a percentage off the original retail price.

By fifth grade, most kids are learning how to do percentages. So, next time you're at the mall, whether you're in a buying or browsing mode, ask them to do the arithmetic on various sale item reductions.

Cover up the sale price of, for instance, a dress. Tell them the original price—$57—and ask them what the item costs marked down 33%. (Answer: $38.19.)

If they need to bring a pocket calculator along, this is fine. The important thing is to get kids comfortable with working with percentages, which is important not only for sales, but for figuring tips and taxes, as well.

Close Enough

Award-winning math teacher Diane Schon Wirtschafter told KQED-TV's Family Services, "Most of the math we do in real life involves estimates, not exact numbers. It's helpful for kids to learn how to 'guesstimate,' and to focus on the skills rather than on answers right down to the penny."

Successful money management involves the skill of estimating. Even the IRS allows taxpayers to round expenses to the nearest dollar.

Ms. Wirtschafter suggests that when shopping with kids ten or older, bring a calculator and have them run a tab of rounded-off prices.

After the cashier presents the actual total, see how close or far off the estimate is.

Opening the Family's Books

It's up to every family to decide how much their kids know or don't know about the household finances.

Many grade-schoolers don't have a clue how much their parents earn—or, in some cases, what exactly the parents do at work.

Other kids, if they learn a parent's salary, may broadcast it (out of either shame or pride) to the immediate world.

Yet, if you want your kids to grow up knowing life's expenses, if you want them to learn financial responsibility, at some point you may wish to openly discuss the families economic picture.

Hopefully, you're a hard-working model of the financial individual you wish your kids to become. You enjoy what money can buy, yet you shop wisely. Being a member of a community, you give money to worthwhile causes, such as your church or synagogue. You save part of your income, and invest another part.

As an activity, have your kids help you draw up a monthly budget.

Give them an idea of household income and its sources. Then present them the necessary expenses: mortgage payment or rent, utilities, phone, taxes, cars, insurance, food, clothes; if applicable, tuition and business supplies or equipment maintenance. Then talk about "discretionary" expenses, such as entertainment, dining out, vacation travel, books, video rentals, and museum memberships.

At the end of a month, see how well the family did.

Not only will your kids learn how to budget their own money, they may very well have a greater appreciation of how hard you work to maintain the family lifestyle.

At The Bank

Make going to the bank a regular errand, like going to the library.

It's important that kids become comfortable in a bank—because banks can be mysterious places. People working there *seem* busy, but what they're doing may not be clear to a kid. And where's the money? Or, more specifically, where's *my* money?

Even more mysterious is how a bank can pay people for their money.

Help your kids understand how a bank can afford to pay interest on savings and other types of accounts.

Explain how a bank takes a kid's twenty dollars and (by adding it to many other customers' savings) turns around and lends it to someone else wanting to buy a house. Explain how the amount a bank charges someone to borrow money (say, at 10% interest) allows it to pay interest to savings customers (say, 4%) and also pay its employees and its own stockholders.

Discuss why keeping money "stuffed in the mattress" is a bad investment. (Because you'll end up with exactly the same amount you started with.)

Aiding The Young Entrepreneur

Helping your kids start their own businesses will be covered in section two of *Kids & Money*—here I want to talk about some of the opportunities available to the young investor.

If your kids like to read the newspaper, one way to wean them away from the comics and sports page is to have them invest their own money in publicly traded securities. Even if a kid owns but a single share—believe me, she'll be checking the business section for the latest trading price on a daily basis.

People choose companies in which to invest for personal reasons. Most often, the company makes a product that the person enjoys. Or the company supports a program that the person likes to watch on TV.

Some companies, particularly if their products or services appeal to kids, have come up with novel programs to attract investors of all ages.

Kelloggs sends all new shareholders a packet of money-off coupons on its cereal products. Tandy, which owns the Radio Shack and Computer City chains, gives shareholders a 10% discount on certain toys, games, and computers. Wrigley's (officially, the William Wrigley Jr. Company) gives shareholders a box of chewing gum at year-end.

A word of caution. If a person is under twenty-one years of age, the parent will need to make the actual stock purchase on behalf of the minor using a custodial account. Any bank or brokerage firm can establish this type of account for you. Or you can buy stock jointly in both your and the child's name.

Once the stock is purchased, you will receive quarterly and annual reports provided by the Investors Services department of the company. It explains how the company is performing and what's in its future plans. It's a good idea to go over the report, even if the graphs and projections may not mean much to your kid until he or she is older.

By the way, you don't have to wait to own shares in a company to receive its annual report. In fact, it's a good idea to receive one *before* you decide whether or not to invest. Companies are always looking for new investors so they give away their annual reports for free—either write or call the company for a copy. Your local library should carry a number of investor's handbooks which give information on companies and their financial history. Among the better known ones are *Standard & Poor's Reports* and *Moody's Handbook of Common Stock.* If you're "on-line," it's likely your service offers up-to-the-minute financial information.

A safe way to "play the market" is by making hypothetical investments. In other words, a kid or a class of

kids start with a set amount of "pretend" money—say, $10,000—and select stocks to invest in, and then track the rise and fall of the stock prices over a period of time.

Schools use this activity by forming teams of would-be Wall Street wizards who first research, then select companies whose stocks are traded on the New York and American stock exchanges and the Nasdaq Stock Market.

The teams are allowed to make transactions. But every transaction "costs" a brokerage fee, which discourages wild trading.

At the end of, say, twelve weeks, the team that's made the most profit is declared the winner.

The Securities Industry Foundation for Economic Education offers its version of "The Stock Market Game" to schools.

If you're interested, contact:

Securities Industry Foundation for Economic
Education
120 Broadway - 35th floor
New York, NY 10271-0280
telephone: (212) 608-1500
fax: (212) 732-6096

Although "playing the market" for real can be lots of fun (and aggravation), no matter how old and savvy you are, for kids in grade school there may be a better way to invest.

Given that an eight year old still has a decade before needing college education, most financial advisors would steer young investors towards long-term investing in growth-stock mutual funds. Over time, these funds, which invest in growing companies, normally stay ahead of inflation and have historically returned in the neighborhood of 10% per year, which most people choose to be automatically reinvested in the form of additional shares purchased in the fund. The key, as with many investments, is to think long-term about the money and let time be your friend.

Some parents are so forward-looking that they help their school-age kids open an IRA (Individual Retirement Account)! To encourage this, consider matching your kid's contribution to the IRA dollar for dollar.

However you help your kids spend/give, save, and invest—remember they must do all three for the World of Money System to work.

As kids get older, they get income from more and more sources. Allowance, for starters, and from odd jobs around the house or neighborhood. It's easy buying a birthday, Christmas or Hanukkah present for an infant, toddler or preschooler—their needs are the same regardless of personality: clothes, toys, books. As a child becomes older, as his or her likes and dislikes seem to shift on a moment's notice, gifts can present a problem. Which may explain why older kids are more likely to receive checks or cash as gifts.

You shouldn't discourage this practice, but remind your kids that gifts of cash or checks are considered income, just like allowance or wages. A gift of money should be divided among Spend/Give, Save, and Invest. It may be a good idea to inform the giver that some of the money will be saved or invested. If your kids write a thank you note, it's a good place to relay this information.

Certainly by the time your kids reach double-digit age, if they are to be successful, good money management must be a habit.

As with other skills, the younger you help your child become a smart consumer, saver, and investor, the higher the likelihood of life-long practice and comfort.

The grade school years may be your best opportunity not only to instill these lessons, but to make the learning fun—for you and your kids.

Mistakes will be made, by both you and your kids. There will be moments of great frustration, followed by moments of great achievement and pride.

Maybe you don't remember the day you and your parents opened the first bank account in your name. When you signed the forms, handed over a sack or envelope of coins and dollars, and received a passbook in a shiny cover. But you'll remember the day you help your grade-schooler open her or his first bank account.

Like other milestones—a child's first word or step, a first haircut, the day the training wheels came off the two-wheel bike—the time spent helping your kids learn how best to manage money will, looking back, become one of the most satisfying memories of parenthood.

Four

"It's Your Own Money, But . . ."

Working With Teenagers

"It's your own money—but you're not going to spend it on that junk!" How many parents have uttered this line to their teenage son or daughter?

Or—"Fine, I'll give you the money to waste with your friends. But this is the last time I give you a loan that I know you have no way to repay."

How about—"It won't be long until you'll be going off to college. Your mother [or father] and I aren't made of gold, if you haven't noticed. So shouldn't you be saving to help with tuition?"

Finally—"You're obviously not interested in my opinion. But do you think piercing jewelry through your nose and dyeing your hair white and purple is the best use of your allowance?"

No question, parenting a teenager is one of life's great—and, hopefully, rewarding—challenges. Some days your teenagers seem so adult, ready to take on the world. Other days, they're as vulnerable as toddlers.

One thing is clear. It won't be long until your teenager is out on her or his own. Which means this may be your last chance to teach them the necessary skills not only to manage their money, but to use it wisely.

If you succeed, one day they'll come back and thank you—even if the likelihood of that gratitude seems as remote as snow in August. If you fail, then they may enter the world as financial illiterates, and face a life of always struggling with too much debt, which translates into a scarcity of opportunity.

Teenagers scare a lot of people, including their parents. But American business loves teenagers, at least teenage workers and consumers.

A recent (November, 1995) edition of *American Demographics* gives some reasons why:

◆ Add the amount of their own money that teens spend to the amount they spend of their family's money and the total equals half of the U.S. defense budget.

◆ 90% of teens are involved in a spending or earning transaction each week.

◆ Two-thirds of teens have savings accounts; nearly 20% have checking accounts; almost one-third of eighteen and nineteen year olds hold a credit card in their own name.

◆ While most adults earn more money than teens, a larger share of teen spending is discretionary (not being saddled with a mortgage helps).

◆ After sixteen years of continuous decline, the teenage population again began to increase in 1992. In 1995, there were 29 million teenagers in the U.S. By 2010, the teen population is expected to reach nearly 35 million.

◆ Nearly half of all teens surveyed say they get their own money "as needed" from parents.

No question, teens have a lot of money and like to spend it. What's sad is how few teens have established the habit of saving or investing. Statistics offered to *Money* magazine by Teenage Research Unlimited (TRU), a Northbrook, Illinois marketing firm, back this up.

TRU surveyed teenagers and found that the average weekly paycheck for a sixteen year old is $51. The average allowance is $33. That makes a total average income of $84, excluding an occasional birthday check from the grandparents. Well, the average sixteen year old spends $62.00 a week—or almost 75% of his or her income!

You'll remember that the World of Money system requires that only two-thirds (not three-quarters!) be allotted for "Spend/Give" and "Save" (which will ultimately be spent). So it's obvious that too many parents are not doing a very good job teaching their teens sound financial habits.

OK, it's clear where the pain is—so what's the cure?

The cure may require you, as parents, to be more open about your financial situation than you've previously been with your teenagers. It may require some new rules. It *will* require that you stop finding excuses not to talk about money with your kids.

If you're willing to openly discuss your own decisions about money with your teenagers, they may very well welcome the candor. If you're willing to treat them as the financially responsible adults they will soon be, you may be pleasantly astonished at the respect you receive in return. So let's begin!

Allowing A Peek Inside The Family Vault

Some parents, who have no qualms about letting their teens take the family car away on a trip, are hesitant to discuss the family finances openly. No one can insist that parents disclose their financial status with their kids, but it is one of the best ways to prepare your teens for the reality of independent living.

Start with what may be the first experience of living outside of the home for most teens: college. For those kids expecting to go off to college after high school, the cost of higher education may be a real eye-opener. The average cost of four years of college tuition has reached $20,000, and this figure includes such "affordable alternatives" as community colleges and state universities. For private colleges or universities, four years of tuition may reach $100,000 or more. More frightening still is that these figures do *not* include room and board, books, supplies, travel, clothing, and entertainment.

Financial educator Neale S. Godfrey tells parents, "Next to a house, a college education is probably the most expensive single item you'll ever pay for."

Almost all teens, except those of the truly wealthy, are expected to help pay for their college years. Even if they receive an academic scholarship, few of these awards pay for non-tuition expenses.

Many parents start a college fund when their kids

are young. If you have such a fund, bring your teens up to date on how much will likely be available when they leave for college, with the understanding that the fund needs to stretch all the way through graduation. This information may help re-orient how they currently spend their money, or propel them toward earning some more.

Now that you have your teens' attention, let's slow down and help them understand a household budget.

In any household, money comes in most often in the following two ways:

◆ salaries or wages

◆ income from investments

Other possible sources of household income may be an inheritance, child support from a previous marriage, or public assistance. Normally, you can estimate pretty closely how much income will come home each month.

Expenses are, understandably, more difficult to estimate. One can't predict, for example, illness, or the furnace breaking, or the spontaneous decision to take the family on an outing. Still, basic expenses include the following:

◆ housing (either a mortgage or rent payment)

◆ groceries

◆ utilities

◆ telephone

- insurance (homeowners or tenants, auto, life; and, if the parents are self-employed, health)

- cars (loan or lease payment, maintenance, gas)

- medical and dental

- charitable donations

- personal care (haircuts, gym memberships, etc.)

- consumer debt payment, if applicable

- entertainment (dining out, movie theater or sporting event tickets, recreational expenses)

- kids' college fund

- a contingency reserve (for the unexpected)

Other possible areas of outlay include an automatic monthly contribution to an Individual Retirement Account (IRA), a mutual fund, or a Christmas Club account at a bank.

Having defined these broad categories, apply the actual amount (or close estimate) to each one. Hopefully, the income exceeds the expenses. If it doesn't, tell your teens what steps you take to stay within a budget.

Finally, and though it's a delicate subject, consider telling older teens about your will. No one wants to die, but kids need to know that you have provided for them, should something happen to you.

Parents, if you don't have a will, you are among the two-thirds of American adults who don't have one, either. But don't take consolation in the size of the companionship, because this majority will be leaving its survivors with an emotional, legal, and financial mess to sort out.

So, as part of a family effort to better manage money, if you haven't done so, contact your attorney and draw up a will. Once it's done, sit down and explain it to your kids. Because your wishes will matter to them.

Now It's Their Turn

Help your teens come up with their individual budgets. Obviously, the categories will vary from the household budget; for instance, most teens do not pay for their own insurance.

For income, include:

◆ Weekly allowance

◆ Job or business

◆ Gifts of cash or checks

For expenses, include:

◆ Savings (remember, this is one-third of income)

◆ Investments (another third of income)

◆ Charitable donations

◆ Food (snacks, school lunches)

◆ Entertainment (movies, video games, sports, CDs or cassettes, dating)

◆ Transportation (public, bicycle, or their own car)

◆ School supplies

◆ Clothing

◆ College fund

◆ Clubs or hobbies

Again, compare the total income against the total expenses. If your teen is ahead of the game, great! If she or he isn't, can expenses be cut down? Or should the two of you consider an adjustment in the allowance amount?

What Should Teens Pay For?

There is no certain answer to this question. It depends on what each family decides for itself.

Parenting guru John Rosemond writes in *Better Homes & Gardens* that he and his wife opened checking accounts for their kids, into which they deposited a monthly allowance.

The Rosemond kids are responsible for all "nonessential" clothing and accessories, like paying the difference if they insist on designer labels. The kids are also responsible for entertainment that doesn't include other family members. If the family goes to the movies, Mom or Dad pays. If the teens go with their friends, the kids pay. The Rosemonds give no loans, which supports the suggestion here not to give kids an advance on their allowance.

Certainly as kids grow older, and their capacity to make money increases, expect them to start paying more of their own way.

Some parents go as far as to charge their older teens rent, particularly if they're home from college for the summer. Although charging your own kids rent may strike some parents as extreme, Teenage Research Unlimited reports that 77% of fifteen-to-eighteen year olds expect to live with their parents until they reach age twenty-four. Charging your kids rent is an extremely personal judgment that you should make on your own.

Janet Bodnar, in *Kiplinger's Money-Smart Kids (And Parents, Too!)*, quotes a recent survey by the American Board of Family Practice which found "a healthy majority of teens said they would be willing to get jobs, buy fewer clothes and give up some allowance to help their families through a financial crunch."

Hopefully, though, self-sacrifice on both the kids' and the parents' part will not be necessary—if a system of financial openness and discipline is in place at the earliest opportunity.

High school graduation is a time of pride. It's a cultural rite of passage, marking a young person's transition from full-time family life to independent living.

Besides witnessing the physical, emotional, and intellectual development of your teenagers, imagine your pride at knowing that you've guided them along the path towards becoming financially intelligent, prosperous adults.

Section Two

Helping Your Kids
Start A Business

Five

Today, A Lemonade Stand. Tomorrow... ?

Getting Started

    Most kids are open to the *idea* of being their own boss. The fantasy of independence and power are appealing. It isn't until the kids realize that running your own business means you're both the Chief Executive Officer (C.E.O.) and bottle-washer that the fantasy loses its luster.

Being an entrepreneur, or someone who takes the risk of starting or taking over a business, is a challenge. It's also a lot of fun, and, if the venture becomes successful, brings with it a rush of pride and a deep sense of accomplishment.

Practical Dreaming

The first thing to help your kids understand before they go out to conquer the world of money are the two simple and necessary "House Rules":

◆ House Rule Number One: No one under the age of eighteen living under this roof can start a business until he or she gets the OK from the parents who are paying for the roof.

◆ House Rule Number Two: Read House Rule Number One!

Why is this so important—besides the fact that the parents may be the start-up business bankers by loaning the young entrepreneur money? How about because it takes the support of family and friends to start and run a successful business.

Any business carries with it the element of risk. But the risk should never be a physical one. In other words, whatever the choice of business, it must be one that is practical and safe.

What type of business is appropriate and practical for kids, but not so appropriate and practical as to be totally boring?

A business won't be successful unless a young person invests enthusiasm as well as time and money. So sit down with your kids and make a list of possibilities.

Start with some basics:

◆ Do you want to work outside or indoors?

◆ Do you want a job that depends on "brawn"—like yard work—or "brains"—like computers?

◆ Do you prefer working with people, or animals—or neither?

◆ Do you want to work by yourself, or with a partner or partners?

◆ Can the business be a first step toward a career later on (like doing yard work now because you want to run a landscaping operation one day)?

We've all had jobs that we hated—usually because the work was boring. Make certain your kids consider something that taps their enthusiasm. Otherwise, it's bound to fail.

Doing The Right Thing

Business ethics is the proper, moral, and legal way a businessperson or commercial venture should operate. The 1980s will be remembered as the decade when business ethics ran into serious trouble. The savings and loan scandal and the insiders trading scandal which rocked

Wall Street and resulted in some of the country's most famous and powerful investors going to prison are but two examples of the decade's sour legacy.

Besides the legal consequences of conducting business in a wrongful manner (stealing from the company, misusing funds, fraudulent record keeping, illegal dumping, covering up a crime, etc.), how might "doing the wrong thing" affect a person individually?

Discuss with your kids if it's worth it if an immediate gain is the result of doing something illegal or morally wrong. What would it be like to lose the trust of others, to have a negative reputation, or be unable to secure a loan in the future?

Now discuss the likely outcome of conducting a business in the right way. How would it affect repeat business, increase trust, and contribute to the building of a successful track record?

One positive reaction to witnessing the results of greed run amok is the current emphasis on teaching business ethics. Most MBA (Master of Business Administration) programs now require a course on ethics, and many high schools incorporate an ethics unit in economics classes.

If you or your kids want to be good business owners, you have to be honest, trustworthy, and hardworking.

You must also follow this rule: *Do the right thing!*

What does this mean? It means trusting your conscience and your values when you have to make a decision. To be honest, doing the right thing can sometimes be the hardest thing to do. And that doesn't change whether you're starting a business at fifteen or fifty! But that's OK, too, because every time we do the right thing, we grow a little stronger.

Safety First

There's an old saying, "An ounce of prevention is worth a pound of cure." If necessary, help your kids understand its meaning.

The following tips and rules may seem obvious. But like most tips and rules, they're worth reviewing *before* your kids start their own business.

♦ Remember House Rule Number One—Don't start a business until your parents give their full approval.

♦ If you are going to use any equipment, read all the manuals and safety tips—and follow the rules!

What are the potential consequences of not learning how to use equipment properly? Well, if it's a lawnmower, it may be a few less toes. If it's a computer, it may be a crashed hard drive or hours of operator frustration.

♦ Dress appropriately for the job you're going to do. For example, if you're working outdoors, wear good quality work gloves, long pants, durable protective shoes, eye protection, and sunscreen.

Why is appropriate dress important? Lawn care guys like to go shirtless and not wear protection for their skin or eyes—sunburn, anyone? How about a scratched cornea? How professional does it look to show up with a torn tee shirt and cutoffs?

This topic should be discussed as an issue of safety *and* decorum.

Would someone want to buy clothes from a salesperson who is a walking fashion disaster? Would you hire someone to take care of your pet if he was scratching himself for fleas? Maybe proper dress *shouldn't* matter, but it *does* matter.

Fairly or not, teenagers lack credibility as business people just because they are young or inexperienced.

Discuss what an ironed shirt, clean hair, and polite manners might do to the image.

Before they start using job-related equipment, tell your kids:

◆ Never, *never*, NEVER operate equipment without an adult showing you how to use it first. And don't use equipment that you are not able to handle safely. If in doubt—ask!

◆ Never put your hands or feet or face near equipment unless the equipment is turned off.

◆ If using a power mower or edger, don't mow or edge around electrical cords or wires.

◆ Never mow over these objects: wire, rocks, wood, limbs, metal, cans, glass, water, and concrete. These can hurt you and your equipment.

◆ Never use gasoline, oil, solvents, or any kind of cleaning material unless you have been instructed by a parent or guardian.

Discuss with your kids that maybe it's a good idea to do a few "freebies" for the family to get the hang of equipment—before they embarrass or hurt themselves trying to make a quick buck elsewhere.

If your kids choose to work in the service area, tell them:

◆ If baby-sitting, go over emergency procedures with the parent hiring you. This includes emergency phone numbers, those of reliable neighbors, the family doctor and the closest hospital; fire escape routes, and how to operate the home security system.

◆ Never leave children in your care unsupervised.

◆ If dog-sitting or dog-walking, always use a leash and collar if you leave a fenced-in yard with the animal. If cat-sitting, know if the animal is an "inside" cat or not; if it is, make certain to respect the owner's instructions when you leave the house.

◆ Take safety classes relevant to your business.

◆ Don't get your friends, brothers, or sisters to help you unless the employer approves and they are able to follow all of these rules, too.

Whatever their business, ask your kids to follow these common sense safety tips:

◆ Always let a family member know where you'll be working before you leave the house. If the rest of the family is gone, leave a note in an obvious place with your schedule and a phone number where you can be reached.

◆ Never approach a stranger unless you are accompanied by an adult.

◆ Keep your money in a safe place. Don't leave it out—ever.

◆ Beware of dogs!

◆ Memorize and practice all of these tips!

If your kids follow all of these rules and tips and use common sense, they should be safe. However, if they find themselves in doubt, they shouldn't do anything that might cause damage to property, equipment, others, or themselves. When in doubt, tell them to *stop and ask first!*

Earlier in the book I discussed the laws governing working minors. Some kids (and grown-ups) may protest that "government shouldn't stick its nose where it doesn't belong." If so, an introduction to *child labor laws* may be useful.

Child labor laws are regulations that define and protect working minors—laws that didn't exist in this country until the early part of the Twentieth Century.

For eons, children have worked in agriculture or were apprenticed to the trades. With the Industrial Revolution of the early Nineteenth Century, kids were viewed as a plentiful source of cheap labor. Girls, many under the age of ten, worked for pennies in the shoe factories and fabric mills of New England. Boys followed their fathers and uncles into coal mines. Sadly, in many countries today, including our own migrant population, children are still exploited for their cheap and servile labor.

In this country, child labor laws grew out of the Progressive Era, a social-political movement of the early 1900s. The government reported in 1910 that over 2 million children were being forced to work to supplement the family income. The children's average wage was less than $2 a week in the clothing industry and less than $3 a week in the very dangerous glass industry. (This pay was less than half of what women were paid. Women, in turn, were paid one-half or sometimes two-thirds less than men doing similar work.)

One government study found that only 20% of boys, some as young as five or six years old, worked *less* than eight hours a day; nearly half (46%) worked ten hours or more.

Boys and girls working in the cotton mills in Fall River, Massachusetts, were twice as likely to contract diseases such as tuberculosis than children not similarly employed.

By 1912, thirty-eight states had passed laws placing restrictions on the age at which children could be employed and the hours which they could work.

So, even though modern kids may resent the law, their health and lives are greatly protected as a result of strict work codes for young people.

Business 101

Before you and your kids go any further, take a minute and ask them this one simple question: *Why do you want to start a business?*

Their answer might be different from these or a combination of several reasons:

◆ Is it to make money?

◆ Do they want to help others?

◆ Is it to save for college?

- Do they want to help the family?

- Are their friends doing it?

- Do they just want something to do with their free time?

- How about all of the above?

A lot of kids are afraid to start a business. But they don't need to be. It's actually a pretty easy thing to do. The trick is to stick with it and help it grow. Actually, that's the trick with just about everything that really matters!

But what if all their fantasies crash and burn? Remind them that almost no one gets it right the first time. Most successful business people have failed, and failed hugely, more than once in their lives. I bet you know a similar story, either about yourself or someone you know.

Sustained effort—steady success. Think about it. The more a person practices at something—the more effort put into it—the better she or he gets at it.

The more you study, the better your grades.

The more you run, the faster your time.

The more you practice guitar, the better you play.

It takes the same kind of patience and practice to develop good business skills. But the rewards can be pretty great, especially the crisp green ones that your kids can claim as their own and spend as they wish.

Strategies For Success

Discuss with your kids their expectations about work. Do they think it's going to be hard—or a day at the beach? Are they worried that they'll never get the chance to just hang out again? Are they concerned that all work and no play will turn them into an android?

To make it easy for themselves—and you—insist that they start slowly: at most, a few hours a week.

A lot of kids start out all fired up to work, work, work. They'll earn the money for that new bike in a week; maybe sooner! That is, if they don't burn out before they drive their friends and family crazy.

Take this business thing easy at first. Make sure that your kids remain focused on school and homework, and that they pursue their regular activities. If they resist, tell them that they have the rest of their life to work, but only a few, short years to enjoy being a kid.

One of the keys to success, in business as well as in life, is to develop good work habits.

Here's a list of good work habits. They should be part of the strategy for succeeding in any activity—including school, clubs, and business.

87

◆ Be on time. Even a few minutes early. And be ready.

◆ Ask questions.

◆ By all means, ask about what you don't understand. There's no better way to endear yourself to an employer than to nicely draw on his or her expertise and experience.

◆ At first, make a list of everything you're supposed to do. When you get comfortable in the job, make the list mental.

You'll be surprised how many little details a business person must keep in her or his head: calls to make, calls to return, supplies to order, supplies to exchange, appointments to make, appointments to reschedule—it's endless!

◆ Be loyal—to your customers, co-workers, family, and friends.

◆ Be friendly and courteous.

Many men still like to be addressed as "sir" or "Mister" and some women prefer "ma'am" or "Ms." Don't be informal until the customer says it's all right to do so.

◆ Do every job for a customer as though you were doing it for yourself.

◆ Budget your time, not just your money.

Help your kids make a weekly schedule, which includes school work, family time, friend time, personal time, and "business"—and help them stick to it!

As they start to get jobs, remind them to block out the times they've committed to customers, and to include a little leeway before and after so they always arrive a little early and have extra time in case the job runs late.

The key is to manage time with the same careful attention that they manage money.

When kids become successful, they may be tempted to flaunt the money they make, or to buy some insanely expensive jacket and hope they'll become the talk of the school. If a jacket props up your kid's ego and makes him or her feel important, so be it. But wouldn't he or she rather put part of their earnings away for something truly special? Or, remembering it's "Spend/Give," not just "Spend"—know that they helped a worthy cause or organization with a contribution?

Tell your kids not to be afraid to seek advice. Most grown-ups (including their parents) like to see youngsters earning their own money. Kids already know that every grown-up loves to give them advice. So pick their brains. Kids don't have to take every bit of advice that they offer, but grown-ups have been around longer and maybe, just maybe, have something to teach about how to improve a business or how to attract more customers.

Every major corporation has a board of directors. A board of directors is usually elected by the shareholders who own the company. The board makes the major decisions which affect the corporation's future plans. The board advises the executives who are in charge of the day-to-day decisions. The point is, everyone needs outside advice, even the C.E.O.'s of major international corporations who are paid millions of dollars.

Every kid knows the fable of the tortoise and the hare. Slow and steady wins the race. It's the same in business. That's why it's important that you encourage your kids to start slowly and work up to more hours, customers, and greater responsibilities. Consistent effort is the key to success.

What if they make too much money, have too much fun, and take over Wall Street? My guess is, you'll be happy to join in. If not, they can always contact me because I may want to hire them!

Setting Some Goals

Setting goals is a very important part of starting a business. Goals are important because if you don't know where you want to go, you'll never get there.

It also helps to write goals down. To make them concrete. To post them and have them as eye-level reminders.

Here's a worksheet for you to do with your kids, to have them write down their business goals.

Remember, goals aren't always just about money. And remember one more thing—goals can change. Kids shouldn't be afraid to set new ones as a business grows and changes.

Goals Worksheet

My goal is to earn $ _____ by _____ so that I can do the following:

1. Spend $_____ on _____
   Spend $_____ on _____

2. Give $ _____ to _____

3. Save $ _____ to buy _____

4. Invest $ _____ in _____

My recommendation is that the above goals include your kids' regular allowance, and that the goals include money that is given to them but not earned with their business.

Many new entrepreneurs start by writing a business plan. (Which I'll ask your kids to do, with your help, in the next chapter.) A business plan outlines the goals and how they'll be achieved. For instance, if someone wants to start a car wash business, the plan will include the equipment needed, how customers will be attracted (through ads or cardboard signs), what each car wash will cost, and how much profit the operator hopes to achieve. The business plan will make projections, which are educated guesses (or "guesstimates") on, in this instance, how many cars can be washed in a given week and at what rate of profit.

If your kids' goals are very ambitious, so ambitious that they'll need to borrow money from you or a bank in order to achieve them—a business plan is essential. No bank, in particular, will loan money to a business lacking a carefully created plan of action.

Whether your kids want to get their feet wet by washing a few cars or dream of monopolizing the lawn care business in your part of town, the process of establishing goals and following basic business rules is the same.

Now, we're ready to teach your kids the fun—and the hard part—which is the actual running of a business.

Six

The Nuts & Bolts
Of Running A Business

Experience is a great teacher. No matter how much preparation goes into planning a business, most of the lessons come from actually running it.

Just as you should expect kids to make mistakes managing their allowance, expect them to goof up from time to time running a business. Remember Murphy's Law, "Whatever Can Go Wrong, Will Go Wrong."

Fortunately, the type of mistakes most young entrepreneurs run into aren't too serious. It's easier for a customer to forgive the neighborhood kid for doing a so-so job on the yard than to forgive an established lawn-care service. Not that kids should feel that running their own business is a game. It isn't. Like any business, it involves money and the consumer's right to expect professional service.

This chapter covers basic operating practices, from getting the business to getting paid.

Getting The Business - Marketing Tips

Marketing is getting the word out about a product or service, in order to attract customers.

No doubt you've been to the grocery store when someone was handing out free samples of chips or juice or cereal. If you liked what you tasted, maybe you were more inclined to buy the item. At the same store, someone else was giving away money-off coupons for other items. Or the store was offering a buy-one-get-one-free sale on still other items. These are examples of marketing. Perhaps a cereal you usually don't buy has your kid's favorite sports star pictured on every box or is offering a mail-back certificate to get a free music CD. This is marketing, as well.

Free samples, coupons, clever packaging, celebrity spokespersons, *premium items* (the certificate for a CD inside the cereal box), advertising, promotion—business people use these and other marketing tools to reach potential customers.

In starting a new business, picking a name is very important. There are successful companies which do nothing but come up with clever names for *other* companies' products. And many graphic design firms specialize in giving companies a distinctive *logo* (commercial symbol, like Apple Computer's famous apple) or color identity. (Quick—what color is a can of Coca-Cola?)

Some businesses pick obvious names, for obvious reasons. If you see a sign for "Gayle's Lawn Care Service," you know what it is about. Some businesses pick witty or even silly names, which bring a smile and describe what it does—for instance, "Curl Up & Dye" for a hair salon. (Or "Hair Port" or "Clip Joint" or "Close Shave" or "Shear Delight"...you get the idea.)

Take a minute and help your kids "brainstorm" possible names for their businesses. Write down the contenders and have your kids decide on the best one. It should be a name they will be proud of, and one that people will remember.

In a nutshell, marketing is doing something that makes people remember you. Why? So they can call on you when they need work done!

As mentioned, advertising is part of marketing. Few kids can afford radio or TV commercials or ads in the daily newspaper—but they can afford other advertising tools like fliers, business cards, and signs. A flier is a single sheet of paper that can be posted, mailed, or handed out.

When time allows, help your kids design a flier for their business. Make it eye-catching, but don't promise more than they can deliver. Make sure to prominently display the business name, the proprietor's (your kid's) name, phone number, and any other important information like hours of operation or pricing.

A tip: Tell your kids not to use the very last flier. Save it so you can make more copies from it when they're ready for more.

Here's a multiple choice question: *What's the best and least expensive way to get new business?*

A. Word-of-Mouth Advertising.
B. Word-of-Mouth Advertising.
C. Word-of-Mouth Advertising.

Did you answer "Word-of-Mouth"? If so, you're absolutely correct!

Almost every kid's first customers are family and neighbors. So tell them to get the word out!

Setting Prices

The key is to charge enough to make a profit, but not so much that you lose the job. Profit is the amount of money left after a business pays its expenses.

A business can't set a price until it has carefully figured its expenses. If the kids haven't estimated their own business expenses—have them do it now. Remind them to include their own time, not just supplies, in figuring expenses.

Once they have an idea of expenses, have them set a price which will allow them a decent (but not outrageous) profit. No customer will spend $50 to have a car washed, given that the expenses are a bucket, a sponge, some soapy water, and perhaps thirty minutes of someone's time.

When business people talk about "what the market will bear," they're discussing the fair pricing of an item or service. In other words, what people are likely to pay without feeling that they are getting "ripped off."

Later on, they may have to make some adjustments to prices, but that's very common for a new business.

If your kids are eager or like the library, have them do some *market research*, which involves learning what similar businesses charge for the same product or service *and* how large the potential customer pool is.

When the kids have an idea of what to charge, discuss these questions:

◆ Should you do a job for less than you normally charge?

Perhaps, if it generates new business.

◆ Should you bargain with a customer?

As long as both parties are happy with the outcome.

◆ What's the advantage—and disadvantage—of offering a range of prices for a range of different services?

The advantage is that customers can select exactly what they want or can afford. One disadvantage is potentially confusing customers and wasting a lot of time clarifying the various levels of service and price.

One last point about prices. A young entrepreneur can try a number of different plans to attract customers:

◆ There's a "first-time discount" to attract the budget-minded.

◆ There's a "referral rate," which means existing customers get a future discount for recommending the business to a friend. Or a new customer gets a discount by mentioning she or he was referred by a present customer.

◆ If a customer is willing to schedule an extended block of time—like an entire summer of lawn care—there can be a "bulk discount" price.

◆ If a customer prepays *and* schedules repeated services, there can be a "super-duper discount" price.

See if your kids can come up with other innovative incentives to get a new customer to give their services a try.

For most businesses, the only sure way to find out what works is to try a variety of pricing alternatives—and keep track of the results.

Put It In Writing

Many jobs—like baby-sitting—normally do not require a contract. But it's a good idea for your kids to use a contract wherever possible, particularly when the work involves a large commitment of their time—for a summer's worth of lawn care, for instance.

Secondly, contracting for work is a good introduction for your kids to the legal world, which all businesses must understand, to some extent.

A contract is a work agreement between two people. In this case, it is between your kids and their customer. Typically, a contract is used to make sure both parties understand what services will be provided, when, and how much they will cost. It's a good idea to get it in writing so that there's not a misunderstanding down the road.

Hopefully, the customer will not be intimidated by filling out a work agreement. After all, it's your kid's promise to perform the exact work that the customer wants, when the customer wants it and at a mutually agreed upon price.

On the next page is a sample work agreement for you to review with your kids. This form can be copied or modified for their own use. Note that the underlined information is what they'll need to customize for each customer.

If a job ends up taking more time than expected or supplies are more expensive than anticipated, can an agreement be amended?

Absolutely, but only *if* the customer is willing. If the customer is not willing, then it's your kid's obligation to fulfill the agreement as originally written.

WORK AGREEMENT

Business Name: _____
Date: _____

1, _____, agree to do the following work to the best of my abilities and 1 guarantee that you will be satisfied:

_____

The above work will be performed on: _____

_____

Security System: __YES__NO   Clean House: __YES__NO
Walk dog:__YES__NO   Prepare meals:__YES__NO

Payment of _____will be received after the work is completed

and approved by _____

Special Notes: _____

_____

Business Owner   Phone Number

Customer   Phone Number

Parent or Guardian   Phone Number

The Pay-Off: Billing For Dollars

At last, your kids' business is up and running. They've found a few customers, agreed on a price, signed the contracts, and performed the work. Now it's time for those dollars to roll in!

Normally (if sadly), a business is paid only *after* the work is completed to the customer's satisfaction. Suggest that your kids don't pack up all of their stuff and leave until they deliver the bill and get paid.

Exceptions to the rule that work is paid only upon completion include when the business must *outlay* (put out) a lot of expenses or time. In these cases, often the payment is split into parts.

For instance, an amount—say, one-third of the total fee—upon starting the job, more upon completing half of the job, and the balance (remainder) when the job is finished to the customer's satisfaction.

An example is a house painter who must purchase paint and may spend days prepping, priming and painting a room. Here, either a *down payment* (part of the fee paid at the start of a job) should be arranged—or the customer should agree to pay for the supplies. Supplies here would be just the paint; not brushes, rollers, tape, throw cloths, ladders, which the painter must buy anyway for his or her business.

To get paid, your kids will need to give their customer an *invoice*. An invoice is also called a "bill." It states what the businessperson did, when it was done, and what amount of money is due. The Work Agreement can be attached, as reference.

An invoice should also include the name of the business and/or the individual getting paid, and an address and phone number. Many businesses number their invoices to help with record keeping.

Your kids should make two copies of an invoice—one to present to the customer and one to keep in their own records.

Have your kids practice making out an invoice, so when they do it for real it will look professional. An invoice is almost always prepared ahead of time, so maybe your kids want to create an invoice form, either on a computer or on paper, which can be customized for each job.

When a business receives payment in full, the invoice should be marked PAID, with the date and a note whether it was by check (write down the check number) or cash—and initialed by the business operator.

The Slow Pay-Off

Nothing is more frustrating than not getting paid for work that was done well and on time.

Hopefully it won't happen, or won't happen very often. But if your kids do not receive the money owed them when they have completed a job—welcome to the wacky world of collections!

Nobody likes to do it, but it's part of being in business. Every business must deal with what is called an "outstanding balance." This type of "outstanding" has nothing whatsoever to do with the good type of "outstanding"—like "outstanding" job or "that meal was outstanding." In financial terms, it means that a customer owes a business money.

There is no magic solution to collections.

One strategy is to avoid any possibility of an outstanding balance by asking for a C.O.D. payment when drawing up the work agreement.

C.O.D. stands for Cash On Delivery. This means the business gets paid the full amount when the product is delivered or the service is provided.

If, however, an invoice is not paid, tell your kids not to jump to the worst conclusion that the customer has no intention of ever paying. Be polite, but persistent. Give the customer the benefit of the doubt—until events convince you otherwise.

Here's the technique I recommend:

◆ Give the customer a couple of days, then go back and ask for payment.

◆ If the customer doesn't pay then, go back again in a couple of days.

◆ If the customer doesn't pay then, go back again in a couple days.

◆ If the customer doesn't pay then, don't do any more work until the account is brought up-to-date—that's your leverage.

Here's the clincher: Each time you go back, leave a collection letter, like the sample on the next page.

YOUR COMPANY NAME

DEAR ,

IT IS MY PLEASURE TO BABY-SIT YOUR CHILDREN. I HAVE WORKED VERY HARD TO DO MY BEST WORK FOR YOU. HOWEVER, FOR MY BUSINESS TO SUCCEED, I MUST RECEIVE TIMELY PAYMENT FOR MY SERVICES. MY RECORDS SHOW THAT YOU HAVE AN OUTSTANDING BALANCE OF _____ . PLEASE PAY IT AS SOON AS POSSIBLE. YOU MAY REACH ME AT _____ AND I WILL GLADLY COME BY AND PICK UP THE PAYMENT.

SINCERELY,

_____   _____
YOUR NAME   DATE

If the collection letter doesn't work, a business person has legal alternatives, but they take time and, unless you happen to have a lawyer acquaintance, money. You can hire a lawyer to write a letter to the customer or even take the customer to small claims court.

If your kids go the legal route, they must be prepared, which means having a copy of the Work Agreement, invoice, proof (if possible) that the work was done professionally and on time, and a record of any past attempts to collect payment.

If your kids find themselves in this awful mess, be sure to tell them one rule: "Above all, don't do anything stupid that gets *you* into hot water."

Welcome To The Paper Trail: Bookkeeping Tips

Every business must keep good records. Records not only tell a business how it's doing, but are essential at tax time to establish annual profit (or loss) and expenses.

In financial terminology, maintaining business records is called "bookkeeping."

Even when your kids are just starting out, they should reserve time every week for bookkeeping. At the least, they need to keep track of their expenses and their income, so they know whether they're "showing" a profit (a gain) or a loss.

Many families have personal computers which come installed with spreadsheet or bookkeeping software, like Quicken. If you have a p.c. with such software, boot up and (assuming *you* know how to run it) show your kids how it works.

If you have a p.c. and don't have the home edition of a spreadsheet software, look for one that can make pie and bar graphs to show, among other things, the percentage of expenses versus the percentage of income. Your kids may find a good visual display easier to understand than a bunch of columns listing numbers.

If you're not yet cruising down the information highway, consider buying your kids an old fashion ledger, which you can find at any office supply store. Or, if you're truly thrifty, you can make up your own ledger, using the forms included in this book.

A good place to start record keeping is with an Equipment/Supply list, like the one on the next page.

Using this form, help your kids write their own business needs, estimate the cost of each item, and then calculate overall operating expenses.

EQUIPMENT / SUPPLY LIST

ITEM	QUANTITY	VALUE

ITEM	QUANTITY	VALUE

(MASTER PAGE! PLEASE PHOTOCOPY!!)

As their businesses develop, your kids will want to complete other bookkeeping records. For example, each month they should list all the jobs they've done, the dates of services, and the amount they received for each job. This record is a Monthly Income Statement, and looks like the one on the next page.

INCOME STATEMENT

Customer	Amount

TOTAL (A) $ [   ]

EXPENSES:
    Equipment/Rental: _____
    Transportation: _____
    Supplies: _____

TOTAL (B) $ [   ]

PROFIT OR LOSS: (Total A - B =) $ [   ]

The young entrepreneur will also want to complete a Monthly Income Statement, which deducts (subtracts) the total amount of expenses from the total amount of income to determine that month's profit or loss.

Here's another way of looking at it:

Income - Expenses = Profit

On the following page is a sample Monthly Balance

Sheet, for your kids to use. The balance sheet will help your kids to list their assets (cash, equipment, inventory, etc.) and liabilities (money owed). Then they will take the total assets and subtract the value of the liabilities to determine the net worth.

Assets - Liabilities = Net Worth

ASSETS: **BALANCE SHEET**

Equipment:

ITEM	VALUE:

TOTAL (A) $ [   ]

SUPPLIES:

ITEM	VALUE:

TOTAL (B) $ [   ]

WHAT YOU OWE:

ITEM	VALUE:

TOTAL (C) $ [   ]

NET WORTH: (A + B - C) $ [   ]

The last basic record keeping form is the Annual Income Statement.

At the end of the year, your kids can calculate an Annual Income Statement to determine the amount of money their business made—or didn't make—for the year.

It'll put the results of a year's blood, sweat, and tears on one page, like the sample below:

ANNUAL INCOME STATEMENT

	INCOME	EXPENSES	PROFIT OR LOSS
JAN			
FEB			
MAR			
APR			
MAY			
JUN			
JUL			
AUG			
SEP			
OCT			
NOV			
DEC			
TOTAL			

if this is positive number, YEAH!!
if this is a negative number, DOOH!!

Secret To Success: Kids, Meet Your Business Plan

We're on the home stretch now!

Helping your kids write a business plan is a terrific way for them to learn more about themselves and their business. Don't believe me? Go ahead, tell your kids to grab a pencil and paper and give it a shot. I bet they—and you—learn something new.

A basic business plan has ten categories, which we'll take one at a time. Parents, remember this is your kids' business, so stand by to answer questions, but let them do this in their own words.

1. MY COMPANY: Kids, write down your company name and then briefly describe your business.

    HINT: The owner must be convincing that she or he has the experience, know-how and enthusiasm to operate this particular business. Do not include information that doesn't pertain to the nature of the business.

2. ALL ABOUT ME: That's right, kids, you're the star. Write a paragraph about YOU. How you got the idea for your business and why you decided to start it. Go ahead and include something about your likes and dislikes. Why? Because a business should express your personality.

3. MISSION STATEMENT: This is the purpose of your business. A Mission Statement outlines what's to be accomplished with a business; in other words, its purpose. It doesn't need to be more than a sentence or two long. No window dressing, just the main, purposeful point.

4. SERVICES PROVIDED: Describe what the business will do for its customers.

    HINT: Don't promise more than you can deliver. But make it clear if you have a way of doing it better than the competition.

5. MARKETING/ADVERTISING: How will you, kids, make others aware of your business? In short, how will you drum up business? Here's where you would list items like fliers and business cards. Don't forget word-of-mouth advertising—it goes here too.

   HINT: Include several concrete examples of a marketing/advertising campaign. Is there any way to get a mention in the newspaper? After all, a news article costs a business nothing and reaches a lot of people. This form of marketing is called *public relations*. And *P.R.* is usually a very cost-effective way to help spread the word about a business.

6. EQUIPMENT/SUPPLY LIST: This is a list of what is needed to operate the business. If you haven't already done one, make it thorough—it all adds up. Make an estimate of the total start-up expenses.

7. FEES/PRICING: What will you charge for your services?

   HINT: Allow for a decent profit, but don't charge so much that you might scare off potential customers.

8. HOURS: Describe how many hours you will put into your new business. As a guideline, most kids do not work more than two hours a day on school days, or more than about a half-day on Saturday. Many kids don't work on Sunday at all. If necessary, stop here and work this out between parents and kids.

HINT: Kids, don't take on more hours than you can handle. You can always add an hour later, but it never looks good to cut back on your hours. Remember, you still have school, home life, time with friends, and other commitments and interests. Also, no one wants someone mowing their lawn at ten at night—so be practical, both with your own time and with the customer's.

9. BUDGET: A list of how much money you will spend and earn. Using the Equipment/Supply list, write down how much money it will take to run the business. Include expenses that do not fall under Equipment/Supply—like phone, wardrobe, lunches, etc. For example, will you have to be driven to your job? If so, should you help pay for gasoline? Here again, it's a good idea for parents and kids to work this out, both so there's an understanding and so the budget amounts will be accurate.

10. FINANCES: Include your Balance Sheet and Income Statement here.

A business plan is not a test. It's a good faith effort in forecasting, so there are no right or wrong answers—just dedication mixed with honest hunches.

Below is a sample business plan that parents and kids can use as a reference.

BUSINESS PLAN FOR TASTY LEMONADE

ABOUT THE COMPANY
Tasty Lemonade is a lemonade stand business in Anytown, USA.

ABOUT THE OWNER
The owner of Tasty Lemonade is TJ Smith. TJ started the business to earn extra money and to learn more about starting and running a business. TJ is twelve years old and attends Anytown School. TJ is honest, trustworthy, and a hard worker. TJ will run Tasty Lemonade safely and profitably.

MISSION STATEMENT
Tasty Lemonade is in business to provide refreshing, tasty lemonade for people in the Anytown, USA, area. By providing excellent, friendly service at reasonable prices, Tasty Lemonade will be a profitable business.

111

MARKETING/ADVERTISING

Tasty Lemonade will get business in two ways:

FLIERS: One-page fliers will be passed out in the neighborhood and posted at the local grocery store and gas station. These fliers will include the business name and location, TJ's name, and phone number.

WORD-OF-MOUTH: TJ will tell everyone about Tasty Lemonade. In turn, parents, friends, neighbors, and relatives will be asked to "spread the word."

EQUIPMENT/SUPPLY LIST

Since TJ's business doesn't own any lemonade stand equipment, TJ's parents have agreed to rent these items to Tasty Lemonade at a rate of .50¢ per day of use:

- One long table
- Two chairs
- Two pitchers
- Two wooden spoons for mixing.

Since TJ is working only in the neighborhood, Tasty Lemonade won't have any transportation expenses—a good way to save even more money!

TJ will purchase these items with savings:
- Business cards
- A ream of paper, for fliers
- Good quality sunglasses (to protect TJ's eyes from glare, strain, and UV rays)
- Sunscreen
- Lemonade

- Large and small paper cups
- Large poster board for Tasty Lemonade sign
- Marker to write on poster board
- Napkins
- First aid kit (just the basics to be safe)

The total cost (investment) for these items is $45.25. This amount is the start-up expense for Tasty Lemonade.

FEE/PRICING

Here is an itemized price list for Tasty Lemonade. Friends and relatives will enjoy reduced rates on some of their lemonade—that's a perk for being related to an entrepreneur!

1.   Large cup of lemonade - fifty cents
2.   Small cup of lemonade - twenty-five cents

HOURS

Four hours each Sat. & two hours a week after school

SAMPLE BUDGET

Projected income and expenses for the first month of operation:

Income:	$120.00
Subtotal:	$120.00
Less: supplies/expenses: (includes start-up)	$45.25
Less: Rent expense:	$ 4.00 (8 days x .50¢)
Total Profits:	$70.75

For our young entrepreneur TJ Smith and Tasty Lemonade—not a bad outing!

Remember, any income—including allowance, gifts of cash, and wages—must be divided among the three components of the World of Money system: "Spend/Give," "Save," and "Invest."

In TJ's case, he divided the $70.75 profit as follows:

◆ $23.59 to "Spend/Give." (For doing such a good job, he gets to spend the extra penny.)

◆ $23.58 to "Save."

◆ $23.58 to "Invest."

Any successful person knows not to rest on his or her laurels. So, TJ (and your kids when they're up and running) needs to review how close he came to his goal after the first month, then make any necessary changes and start planning for the rest of the year.

So, there's the nuts and bolts of operating a business. The next chapter offers some tried-and-true and some novel business ideas for kids.

Seven

"You Mean I Can Make Money Doing *That*?"

Business Ideas for Kids

Besides the obvious candidates like baby-sitting, dog walking, car washing, and mowing lawns, there are a lot of ways for kids to augment their allowances by earning their own money.

This chapter offers business opportunities that kids can do without a lot of training or expense.

The Used Book Merchant

Families should build and maintain their own household library. But not every book we buy or receive belongs in a collection. Some may be picture books which no longer appeal to older kids. Some may be paperbacks bought for last summer's vacation. If you have books which are merely taking up space and gathering dust, they also represent a business operation for a young entrepreneur.

Almost every community has a book exchange that buys used books at a fraction of their original cost and which pays cash for titles it wants for its inventory.

Parents, go through the house with your young book merchant and give him or her any titles you no longer want. Kids, ask neighbors, friends, and relatives to do the same.

An understanding needs to be negotiated as to whether the merchant will split the income from any sale of the books with the original owner, or if the merchant gets to keep all of the loot. Regardless, any income from the business should be divided among the "Spend/Give," "Save," and "Invest" system outlined earlier in this book.

(By the way, if you've truly extracted every bit of information and advice from this book, go ahead and sell it. My hope, though, is that you'll want to keep it around for future reference.)

SUPPLIES/EXPENSES: Nominal. Gas to and from the book exchange. If the business expands, fliers and business cards.

PROFIT POTENTIAL: Modest to high.

Younger Sibling Tutor

If you're a multi-kid family, chances are the older kids can help the younger kids with homework, and give the parents a little break.

Now, you may consider this assistance as something that should be granted freely. If, however, you have no qualms about paying an older sibling for helping, work out a fee arrangement payable in twenty-minute increments. (Many younger kids' attention spans or home-work requirements do not exceed twenty minutes.)

Parents should be available to monitor this, and to guard against the older sibling enjoying his or her authority a little too much.

SUPPLIES/EXPENSES: None.

PROFIT POTENTIAL: Modest. No expenses is a good thing; but, at best, this job may be good for only a few hours a week.

Vivid Videographers

For the older teen, experienced with operating a video camcorder, there's a business in recording kids' birthday parties for their busy-elsewhere parents.

At many parties where grown-ups are outnumbered by excited, sometimes rowdy kids, it would help to have someone responsible for the video camera. It's a good idea to know whether the customers want a series of party highlights or if they want most everything recorded so they can edit the tape themselves later.

The fee could be by the hour, if the entrepreneur uses the customer's camcorder and does no editing. Additional services could include editing and special packaging.

SUPPLIES/EXPENSES: Rental of a video camcorder, blank tape cassettes; gas to and from the party.

PROFIT POTENTIAL: Modest to high.

Good Paper Goods

If creative, kids can make and sell their own line of greeting cards and wrapping paper.

Kids can draw graphics and pictures themselves or search for graphics in old magazines and catalogs and cut out or copy the artwork.

The cards themselves should be made of good card stock, available at a stationery or arts supply store. Envelopes can be made too! The wrapping paper could be colored butcher paper, also available at arts or craft supply stores.

Of course, holidays are a time when people are looking for distinctive cards to send to friends and family. So the entrepreneur should have a range of Christmas, Hanukkah, New Year's, Valentine's Day, Easter, and Passover cards. Every year brings birthdays, anniversaries, graduations, so these occasions should be included in any card line. In addition, there are such standard sentiments as friendship, love, get well, and bon voyage, which people like to communicate with cards.

To save money, the entrepreneur's inventory of different styles should be for display purposes only. In other words, don't make additional cards or wrapping paper until first obtaining a customer's order.

SUPPLIES/EXPENSES: Arts and craft supplies: card stock or butcher paper, glue, scissors, etc., and blank envelopes for the cards.

PROFIT POTENTIAL: Modest.

Hey, Hey, I'm A D.J.

Another idea is to help out at busy parties by providing the music. If it's a little kids' party, they'll want
to play Musical Chairs. If it's an older kids' party, they
may want to get up and dance. If the party is for parents, a little rock and roll nostalgia may be in order.

The key is to make certain that the party music match-
es the customer's need. So, before party day, the entrepreneur needs to know what type of music to bring.
Before arriving at the party, "cue up" specific songs (if
using cassettes) so there's no time wasted searching for
a particular tune.

For the service, charge a fee based on the length of
the party.

Warning: a collection of compact discs covering a
range of musical taste can cost hundreds of dollars. One
way to avoid a high inventory cost is to borrow CDs
from your local library or to "rent" them from parents
or friends—or use those of the person having the party.

SUPPLIES/EXPENSES: A portable tape or CD player,
party tune tapes either pre-recorded, bought or borrowed.

PROFIT POTENTIAL: Modest.

It's Carnival Time

Families love back yard carnivals. It's a chance to get everyone out of the house, a chance for kids to get their faces painted and their fortunes told, and for parents to either participate or have a good time watching.

Either alone or with friends, the young entrepreneur can plan, market, and run a neighborhood carnival. Marketing is absolutely essential. For a carnival to succeed, there must be a crowd, to create an air of excitement. So, several days before the carnival, post signs and deliver fliers around the neighborhood.

A back yard carnival can be as simple as a face-painting booth and a table selling lemonade and cookies. An easy "game of skills" is a balloon toss. Fill a balloon with water, tie off the end, and have two contestants toss it back and forth: first standing close together and, with every toss, taking a step backwards. The one who does *no*t have the balloon burst on him or her is the winner, who can receive an inexpensive prize. (The loser can receive the use of a towel.)

If ambitious, build ball-toss and dunk-the-clown booths, give away prizes, and serve hot dogs and slices of pizza. Obviously, the more complicated, the higher the expenses and the higher the potential for profit.

SUPPLIES/EXPENSES: Fliers, signs. Face paint, snacks, script (paper tickets).

PROFIT POTENTIAL: Moderate to High.

Cookies, Cookies, Cookies

Bake sales are a good business for the young entre-preneur—assuming the product is tasty.

To guarantee quality, the business can buy baked goods from a professional bakery, then up the price a bit in exchange for delivering them to the customer's door. Or, if there's a good baker in the family, the business can operate out of the kitchen, and maximize the profit.

EXPENSES/SUPPLIES: Baked goods, order forms, de-livery supplies (bags or boxes, gasoline).

PROFIT POTENTIAL: Low to moderate.

The Baby-Sitters Club Booker

A lot of kids like to baby-sit, but many don't like to seek out jobs. Conversely, parents aren't sure who to call if their regular baby-sitter isn't available.

The idea here is to provide one place for parents to call to find a qualified baby-sitter.

For this business to work, a young entrepreneur needs to canvas his or her friends and ascertain their availability to baby-sit after school or on the weekends. Once a schedule is completed, the entrepreneur can "book" jobs for the network of sitters as parents call up.

CAUTION: This will work only if the baby-sitters and the customers know and trust each other. Which means the sitters and the customers need to be carefully matched up by the booking agent.

CAUTION: All jobs must be approved by parents, but this one especially. The phone may ring and ring, as weekends approach, so even the installation of a second telephone line may be necessary.

The agent receives a commission—say, 20%—of the sitter's fee. Some sitters may not like this, but they might not be working if not for this centralized service.

EXPENSES/SUPPLIES: Telephone, fliers, business cards.

PROFIT POTENTIAL: High.

Photo Album Organizer

This one is geared toward a kid earning some extra money from his parents.

How often do snapshots come back from the processor only to sit around in their folder until they are misplaced or lost? What if someone took the responsibility of sorting and organizing the photos, and keeping the family album up-to-date?

The good photo scout will toss out the over- or underexposed or out-of-focus shots, and organize the good ones in chronological order.

SUPPLIES/EXPENSES: None.

PROFIT POTENTIAL: Modest.

Parent Computer Tutor

In most homes, the kids are more comfortable with the family personal computer than the parents are.

Even if it's just learning a game or doodling in an electronic art studio, it might be nice for the kids to teach the parents a thing or two.

SUPPLIES/EXPENSES: None.

PROFIT POTENTIAL: Moderate.

Halloween Haunts

With the parents' permission, of course, a basement or garage could be turned into a haunted house at Halloween.

Again, marketing is essential, as the entrepreneurs should have an idea of how many people to expect. If ticket sales are brisk, don't be afraid to spend more money on decorations. If ticket sales are frighteningly slow, best cut back on expensive plans.

CAUTION: Nothing should be so scary that young trick-or-treaters run home in terror. For safety sake, the haunted house *must* have some light. Young customers should be warned about scary parts, and no one should be forced to go through the house.

Sometimes, the easiest trick is the scariest. Put a bowl of cold, cooked spaghetti in a box that has an opening only large enough to slip a hand through. When the customers touch the spaghetti, tell them it's cold brains. Gross!

SUPPLIES/EXPENSES: Fliers, tickets, costumes, decorations, and spaghetti.

PROFIT POTENTIAL: Moderate, short-term.

Keeping An Empty House Company

When people go away on business travel or vacation, a business opportunity exists for young entrepreneurs. They can take in the mail, water the plants, take garbage bins to the curb on collection day, turn lights on and off, and other domestic services.

When people go out of town, they have to make

arrangements for their pets. Many people take dogs and cats to a kennel, which can be expensive. But, if the pets are used to being kept inside, the young businessperson can offer to put out food and water, and to walk dogs, while providing the other services.

The opportunities may be not be weekly, but this job could be scheduled around school, activities, chores, and other jobs.

The jobs may not come immediately, but if neighbors know that a responsible young person is available, the phone will ring with job offers.

SUPPLIES/EXPENSES: Fliers, business cards.

PROFIT POTENTIAL: Moderate.

Snow Job

When it snows, everyone with a shovel seems ready to make a few dollars clearing a neighbor's walks or

driveway. Other wintry services are shaking the snow off trees and bushes and clearing snow off cars and scraping the ice from windows.

The trick, though, is to "pre-sell" a winter's worth of shoveling before the flakes fall. The customers will be glad to know someone else will be responsible all winter long, and the entrepreneur will know his or her income before the first frost. The risk, of course, is if it's a particularly harsh winter, the entrepreneur will be buried in snow, not profits.

SUPPLIES/EXPENSES: Shovel, warm clothes.

PROFIT POTENTIAL: Moderate to high.

Obviously, there are many more business ideas for kids.

The key is for your kids to look around the neighborhood and see what services or products people need. In other words, they should do some market research.

Then they must market to those needs, to let potential customers know that there's someone willing to help out and to do so at a reasonable cost. But kids should do jobs that interest them, too—because they'll do a better job and have more fun if the work is important to them.

Finally, they must perform the work professionally, which is the surest way to keep existing customers and to attract new ones through word-of-mouth.

Chances are, the lessons kids learn from running their first business will stay with them for the rest of their lives.

Conclusion

Welcome to the World of Money

So now you have the World of Money system.

The principles are simple. If you and your kids follow the system as outlined in the first part of this book, they will be well on their way to learning how to manage money. And this is no small feat.

Managing money is consistently one of the hardest things any of us will ever have to do. So, if at first your kids find it downright difficult, they're in good company.

We all struggle with money at times. We overspend or discover we were unnecessarily frugal. We get "ripped off" by unscrupulous businesses, or we cheat ourselves by buying impulsively and not comparison shopping and waiting for sales.

The lessons that our kids learn about money may not come easily—but which lessons about life do? Be patient with them; and, in return, ask that they be patient with you.

Any change in the family may take a long time to implement and a longer time to properly assess its success or failure. At the start, you'll have to remind your kids about the rules—for instance, about always splitting their income into the three components of "Spend/Give," "Save," and "Invest." You may have to fund the start of their business and offer to help them through slow periods. For a while, you may be their only customer!

Keep in mind, discipline is essential. Managing money is hard work, but it also can be a lot of fun. There's nothing more satisfying than enjoying money you've worked hard to earn or watching investments grow in value.

The effort is worth it—because you'll be doing your kids the ultimate service if you send them out into the world as financially responsible individuals.

Glossary

advertising - publicity a business or person has to pay for. Examples include cards and brochures, commercials, billboards, and newspaper or magazine ads.

allowance - a set amount of cash given to kids by their parents on a regular basis; part of kid's income, along with jobs and gifts of cash.

annual report - the published, yearly financial statement of a company; free to shareholders and potential investors.

assets - anything of value to an individual or company, such as cash, equipment, or an inventory of goods.

balanced budget - when the amount spent does not exceed the amount received, saved or invested.

balance sheet - a list of all assets and liabilities (money owed). When you take the total of your assets and subtract the value of your liabilities, you determine your *net worth*. (Assets - Liabilities = Net Worth.) Your balance sheet is a written document of these values.

bank - a business which keeps customers' money safe and pays them in order to lend the money to other people needing to borrow it in the form of a loan.

bankruptcy - when a person or company has so little cash and owes so much money that he/she/it cannot pay his/her/its bills and is legally declared insolvent (broke).

bookkeeping - the practice of maintaining written records of your financial transactions.

bottom line - the amount of an individual or company's current profit or loss.

break even - in a business, the point where profits equal expenses.

budget - a plan of how much to spend, and how much to save and invest.

business plan - a document describing a new money-making venture, including its mission statement, its product or services, estimated start-up costs, projected prices and profits, and short- and long-term goals.

capital - money used in business.

certificate of deposit - a banking product in which a certain amount of money is left undisturbed in the bank for a specific time period.

check - a written order to a bank (or other financial institution) to take money from one's account in order to pay for a product, service or debt.

child labor laws - federal and state laws that protect working minors.

contract - a written agreement between two people: one providing a service or product, the other paying for it.

credit - money borrowed that must be repaid in the future, usually with an additional charge for the loan.

credit card - a small plastic card, issued by a financial institution, to allow a customer to make purchases on credit. Credit cards normally carry with them very high interest charges, which go into effect if the credit balance is not paid in full and on time.

creditor - someone to whom money is owed.

currency - anything used and accepted as a medium of exchange. Today, currency means money—but in the past it included precious minerals or stones, shells, feathers, and salt.

customer - a person or entity paying for a service or product.

debt - money owed.

deposit - money put in a bank, to be held for future use or investment.

dividends - company or corporation profits distributed to its shareholders.

earnings - profit. The total of your income minus your expenses.

economics - the study of a society's business, financial, and consumer history and habits.

entrepreneur - a person who starts a business or who assumes the risk of operating a business.

expense - the cost of doing business. Expenses can include time as well as money.

fee - the amount of money charged to a customer for a service.

finance - the world of money, banking and investments.

fliers - single sheets of paper that advertise a product or service. Fliers can be mailed (with permission), posted or simply handed out door-to-door.

goal - what one wishes to accomplish.

guarantee - a binding promise, either written or oral, to deliver a specific service or product, at an agreed price.

income - money received from providing a service or selling a product.

income statement - a financial document that shows income minus expenses over a period of time.

income tax - money that goes to the federal, state or local government to pay for public services; based on a percentage of one's net income over a year's time.

interest - 1.) profit given by a bank to savings accounts in exchange for keeping the money on deposit; or 2.) a charge added to the cost of borrowing money (loan).

Internal Revenue Service (IRS) - the federal agency in charge of collecting income tax from individuals and corporations.

inventory - a supply of products, ready to be sold.

investment - money put into a stock, bond, mutual fund, or items like coins, stamps, a house, and left alone until the initial outlay of capital has grown in value.

invoice - a written request to be paid for services or product provided.

loan - money borrowed, to be paid back, usually at a higher cost than the original amount.

loss - when expenses are greater than income.

market - a target group of potential customers.

mission statement - a brief statement outlining the purpose for which a business was created.

money-market accounts - a type of savings account with special rules, such as a minimum deposit and maximum number of withdrawals per month. In exchange for stricter rules, this financial product pays higher interest than normal savings accounts.

mutual fund - a financial product in which a lot of people pool their investment money to collectively buy stocks and bonds.

net worth - one's financial standing. Subtract liabilities (what you owe) from assets (what you own, like cash, property valuables).

outlays - the spending of money; in business, for such

things as supplies, salaries, utilities, phone, and supplies.

overhead - fixed costs of operating a business, such as rent, salaries, utilities, phone, and supplies.

plan - a list of purposeful steps taken to reach a goal.

portfolio - an individual's or company's group of investments

price - the cost of an item. *Wholesale price* is what the manufacturer charges a store. *Retail price* is what the store charges a customer. The store makes its profit on the difference between the wholesale and retail price —this profit is called the mark up.

price list - an inventory of what a business charges a customer for specific services or products.

profit - amount of money left after a person or company pays expenses.

profit and loss statement - another term for Income Statement.

prospect - someone you would like to have become a customer.

receipt - a written document showing money received for services or goods. Commonly used when customers pay with cash. A canceled check (one that's been cashed or deposited at a bank) serves as a receipt, too.

records - written documents that show a business's activities and its profits or losses.

refund - money given back to a customer when a product is returned, or when the customer is unhappy with a service or product.

revenue - money a person or company receives in payment for services or products.

salary - the amount of money a person is paid to do a job, on an annual (yearly) basis.

service - work offered to a customer.

share - a single unit of ownership in a company or corporation.

Social Security Number - identification number assigned to an individual by the federal government. It's used for, among other things, taxes and tracking finances.

start-up - the amount of money needed to open a business.

stock - 1.) a certificate of ownership in a company or corporation; sold in shares; and 2.) in business lingo, the inventory of product on-hand, usually kept in the "stockroom."

tax - a government fee added to consumer products and taken from individual and business income, to pay for public services.

tax return - an annual income report prepared on a specific form, to the state and federal governments, which determines how much tax is owed, based on income, to the state or federal treasury.

unemployed - out of work.

wages - what a person is paid to do a job, on an hourly basis.

Wall Street - name of an actual street and a district in Lower Manhattan, in New York City, where the New York Stock Exchange and other financial headquarters are located.

withdrawal - removing money from a bank account or mutual fund.

work agreement - a contract between a customer and a business owner that specifies work to be performed and at what cost for a customer.

Bibliography

Resources For Parents:

Recent Books:

Barbanel, Linda. *Piggy Bank to Credit Card: Teach Your Child The Financial Facts of Life.* New York: Crown, 1994.

Blue, Ron, and Judy Blue. *Raising Money-Smart Kids.* Nashville: Thomas Nelson, 1992.

Bodnar, Janet. *Kiplinger's Money-Smart Kids (And Parents, Too).* Washington: Kiplinger, 1993.

Drew, Bonnie, and Noel Drew. *Fast Cash for Kids.* Hawthorne, NJ: Career Press, 1991.

Estess, Patricia Schiff, and Irving Barocas. *Kids, Money & Values: Creative Ways to Teach Your Kids About Money.* Cincinnati: Betterway Books, 1994.

Godfrey, Neale S. *Money Doesn't Grown On Trees: A Parent's Guide To Raising Financially Responsible Children.* New York: Fireside, 1994.

Lewin, Elizabeth, and Bernard Ryan. *Simple Ways To Help Your Kids Become Dollar-Smart.* New York: Walker, 1994.

Schmatjen, Judith A. *Kids 'N' Cash: How To Raise Money-Wise Children.* Sacramento: Tzedakah Publications, 1995.

Recent Articles:

Bodnar, Janet, "Money Matters," *Parents*, May, 1995: 68-70.

Bowe, Claudia, "Money Matters: What To Teach Your Kids About Cash, *Redbook*, October, 1994: 186-190.

Branch, Shelly, "How To Teach A Teen The Value Of A Buck," *Money*, December, 1995: 136+.

Edelman, Gay Norton, "What Kids Need To Know About Money," *Working Mother*, January, 1995: 42-46.

Gray, Charlotte, "Teenage Money Management: How To Encourage Financial Responsibility," *Chatelaine*, December, 1994: 24.

Hoyt, Carolyn, "Gimme! Gimme!" *McCall's*, Dec., 1995: 132-136.

Rosemond, John, "Kids And Money," *Better Homes & Gardens*, October, 1995: 36.

Spragins, Ellyn E., "Kids And Their Cash," *Newsweek*, October 2, 1995: 68-69.

Internet Web Sites:

World of Money
http://www.worldofmoney.com

Family.com.
http://www.family.com

Kids' Money, by David McCurrach.
http://pages.prodigy.com/kidsmoney

Kids Finance Home Page, by the San Jose Education
Network. http://www.sun.sjen.org

KQED's Family Services.
http://www.kqed/org/fromKQED/cell/famhome.html

Parents Place, by The National Parenting Center.
http://www.parentsplace.com

Parents Soup. http://www.parentsoup.com

Appreciate that new Web sites appear daily—and old
sites *disappear* almost as often.

Use your Web browser to find relevant sites by using
such terms as "Kids" "Money" "Parents & Children"
"Financial Advice" and "Kids Economics".

Resources For Kids

Recent Books:

Banks, Ann. *It's My Money.* New York: Puffin, 1993.

Berg, Adriane G., and Arthur Berg Bochner. *The Totally
Awesome Business Book for Kids.* New York:
Newmarket, 1994.

Berger, Melvin, and Gilda Berger. *Round And Round
The Money Goes: What Money Is And How We Use
It.* Nashville: Ideals Children's Books, 1993.

Bernstein, Daryl. *Better Than A Lemonade Stand.* Hillsboro, OR: Beyond Words, 1992.

Berry, Joy. *Every Kid's Guide To Intelligent Spending.* Chicago: Children's Press, 1988.

Johnson, Anne Akers. *The Buck Book: All Sorts Of Things You Can Do With A Dollar Bill Besides Spend It.* Palo Alto: Klutz Press, 1993.

Maestro, Betsy. *The Story of Money.* New York: Mulberry, 1993.

Spies, Karen Bornemann. *Our Money: The History, Minting And Use Of Money In The United States.* Brookfield, CT.: Millbrook Press, 1992.

Thompson, Terri. *The Barron's Biz Kids' Guide To Success.* Hauppauge, NY: Barrons, 1992.

Wyatt, Elaine, and Stan Hinden. *The Money Book: A Kid's Guide to Savvy Saving And Spending.* New York: Tambourine Books, 1991.

Index

Safety, 81-84
Sales, 56
Savings, 23-29
    accounts, 25-26
    national rate, 3, 25
    need to teach, 25
    teen rate, 21
Seven to twelve year olds. 47-
    63
    spending by, 21
Shopping, 22
    activities about, 43
    with preschoolers, 36-38
Social Security Number, 50
Spending, 20-23
    by teenagers, 64-66
    learning about, 43-46
Spend/Give, 20-23
Stamp collecting, 28, 54
Stock market, 59-62
Stock Market Game, 61
Stocks, 30, 59-62

Taxes, 33
Teenagers, 64-72
    income of, 2, 65-67
    influencing parents, 2
    spending by, 2, 20-21, 70-71
Television,
    advertising, 5
    effects on preschoolers, 44-
    46
Thirteen to eighteen years old.
    See *Teenagers*

U.S. Mint, 53

Wall Street, 61, 80
Wills, 69-70
Work agreement. See *Contracts*

Work habits, 85-90
World of Money Three-Part
    System, 19-29, 62-63, 127-128

About The Author

Michael J. Searls is the President and CEO of Summit Financial Products, Inc. and creator of the World of Money line of products which teach people of all ages about successful money management.

Prior to creating World of Money, Searls was a prominent Wall Street investment advisor. He has won numerous broker awards including "Broker of the Year" and was in the nation's top 5% of brokers for many years. He has been featured on Financial News Network, National Business Radio, CNN, CNBC and is an acknowledged expert on kids and money.

Searls received a business administration degree from Wichita State University in 1982.

Searls' World of Money product line, including the best-selling World of Money Allowance Kit, is selling in toy and book stores across the nation.

Searls, his wife Lisa, and their four children live in Parker, Colorado

Other WORLD OF MONEY Products

To order or to find a local retail store, call
1-800-FOR-A-KIT (1-800-367-2548)

WORLD OF MONEY ALLOWANCE KIT

A hands-on, three-part money management system designed to teach children ages 7 to 14 how to spend, give, save, and invest. This concept has never before been packaged, and contains all the tools necessary to guide kids--and their parents--through the principles of successful money management.

The Kit includes a three-part Allowance Kit bank, a colorful handbook, stickers, locks, an audio cassette, a chore list, an investment register and lots more.

While learning the value of a dollar, kids develop the skills that lead to future financial independence...in a way that is easy-to-understand, interactive, and most important, fun!

WORLD OF MONEY ALLOWANCE KIT JUNIOR

The Allowance Kit Junior is a simplified version of the Allowance Kit and is designed for children ages 3 to 7. Here, the bank is color-coded like traffic lights: the green component is "spend," the yellow "save," and the red, stop and "invest." The Junior kit comes with a quick-start guide, stickers, locks, an audio cassette, and more.

WORLD OF MONEY BUSINESS KITS FOR KIDS

World of Money Business Kits For Kids are business start-up and management systems for kids 12 and older, which provide hands-on tools that make learning how to run a real business fun and educational.

Currently, there are five World of Money Business Kits for Kids, with more on the way.

1. Standard Edition (general business)
2. Lawn-Mowing
3. Baby-Sitting
4. Pet Care
5. Car Wash

Each Business Kit for Kids comes complete with a handbook, a supply of business cards, fliers, and invoices; and a video tape which walks through the system with interesting facts and helpful hints on how to get in business and stay successful.

WORLD OF MONEY POCKET BANK

Pocket Bank is a portable money management system which teaches children ages 4 and up about the basic principles of spending, giving, saving, and investing. The three-compartment wallet and calculator provide the tools with which to manage money while kids are on-the-go!

In addition to a wallet and calculator, each Pocket Bank comes with an instructional audio cassette.

WORLD OF MONEY KID'S CALCULATOR

The portable World of Money Kid's Calculator will help kids manage money wherever they are. The handy string makes traveling with the calculator easy!

WORLD OF MONEY "THE BUCK STARTS HERE" PROGRAM

"The Buck Starts Here" is the classroom edition of the Allowance Kit money management system. This educator's manual is designed to teach kids ages 7 to 14 about the value of a dollar and the important elements of successful money management. The program is sold as a package and comes complete with:

1. Teacher's curriculum
2. Video
3. Ten Allowance Kit systems

WORLD OF MONEY "THE BUSINESS STARTS HERE" PROGRAM

"The Business Starts Here" is the classroom edition of Business Kits for Kids. The program is a course designed to teach kids ages 12 and up about all aspects of starting and running a business.

The program is sold as a package and comes complete with:

1. Teacher's curriculum
2. Video
3. Ten Student Packs, which include handbooks, fliers, business cards, and invoices.

For information about any World of Money product, call:

1-800-FOR-A-KIT (1-800-367-2548)